Guided by an Unseen Hand:

How to Detect God's Involvement

in Our Everyday Lives

by
Oscar J. Daniels, Sr.

TEACH Services, Inc.
P U B L I S H I N G
www.TEACHServices.com • (800) 367-1844

World rights reserved. This book or any portion thereof may not be copied or reproduced in any form or manner whatever, except as provided by law, without the written permission of the publisher, except by a reviewer who may quote brief passages in a review.

The author assumes full responsibility for the accuracy of all facts and quotations as cited in this book. The opinions expressed in this book are the author's personal views and interpretations, and do not necessarily reflect those of the publisher.

This book is provided with the understanding that the publisher is not engaged in giving spiritual, legal, medical, or other professional advice. If authoritative advice is needed, the reader should seek the counsel of a competent professional.

Copyright © 2016 Oscar J. Daniels, Sr.

Copyright © 2016 TEACH Services, Inc.

ISBN-13: 978-1-4796-0573-6 (Paperback)

ISBN-13: 978-1-4796-0574-3 (ePub)

ISBN-13: 978-1-4796-0575-0 (Mobi)

Library of Congress Control Number: 2016904137

The contents of this book are protected by copyright registration number TXu 001-939-754.

All rights are reserved by the author.

Cover art by Harry Anderson.

Used by permission of the Review and Herald Publishing Association.

All scripture, unless otherwise noted, is taken from the King James Version. Public Domain.

Scripture quotations marked (RSV) are taken from the Revised Standard Version of the Bible, copyright © 1946, 1952, and 1971 the Division of Christian Education of the National Council of the Churches of Christ in the United States of America. Used by permission. All rights reserved.

Published by

TEACH Services, Inc.
PUBLISHING
www.TEACHServices.com • (800) 367-1844

Table of Contents

Foreword..v

Chapter One
The Early Years...7

    My Spiritual Growth Reaches a Whole New Level of Maturity........ 15

    Some Basic Bible Doctrines Seen in a Whole New Light--
    the Light of God's Word and History 18

    Which Day is the Sabbath Day Chosen by God, and Did He Ever
    Change It?... 18

    When and by Whom was the Sabbath Day Changed from
    Saturday to Sunday?.. 25

    The Ten Commandments 27

    What Happens to Us When We Die? 28

    God's Commandment Concerning Giving 32

    The Adventist Church Becomes My Big and Wonderful
    Extended Family 33

Chapter Two
I Love Pittsburgh, PA 37

Chapter Three
College, Career, and Family..41

    College Days... 41

    The Start of My Career with the Job of My Dreams 51

    Military Service: God Uses the Army to Open Up Whole New
    Worlds for Me.. 55

    Courtship and Marriage 59

    Our European Adventure:
    God Enables Us to Fulfill Our Dreams—He'll Do the Same for You .. 65

    Returning to College to Complete Some Unfinished Business 77

    Parenthood: Our First Child Is Born 78

    A Trans-Canadian Journey to Alaska 82

    God Opens the Windows of Heaven
and Pours Out Multiple Job Opportunities 88

    South of the Border, Down Mexico Way 90

    Wilma's Amazing Parenting Skills. 92

    Winter Wonderland: A Week at a Ski Resort. 95

    The Children Find Their Place in the World, and I Enter My Golden
Years Still Guided by God's Unseen Hand 96

Chapter Four
Observations and Conclusions After a Retrospective Look at My Life . . . 99

    Finding Something Good in Everything 99

    Six Life Principles. 104

    How to Maintain the Flow of God's Blessings Into Your Life 108

A Tribute to My Many Mothers 119

Endnotes 123

Foreword

No matter where I go, says the psalmist, "… thy hand [shall] lead me" (Psalm 139:10). His son, King Solomon, is said to be the wisest man who ever lived, and so we can learn from and rely upon his insights. In Proverbs 3:5 and 6, he reveals how to obtain God's guidance in our lives. He says, "Trust in the Lord with all of your heart, and lean not upon your own understanding. In all of your ways, acknowledge him, and he will direct your paths." Those words are not just a nice-sounding philosophical expression. They are absolute truth. When we apply to our lives the principles that Solomon taught us, we can be assured of God's guidance in our lives. There is no better, more fulfilling, and more stress-free life that we can have than one that is guided by God's unseen hand. In this book, you will learn how to look for and detect God's guidance and direct involvement in your everyday life.

The Lord is continually bringing into our lives the people and experiences we need in order to prepare us for the next phase of our lives. Often, we are all so engaged in our day-to-day activities that we don't recognize his involvement. I'm going to briefly tell the story of my life and provide a few examples that show evidence of his involvement. You can decide whether they are mere chance occurrences or something more.

Like most people, I wasn't consciously aware of God's direct involvement in my life on a daily basis until I was in my seventies and decided to take a retrospective look at my entire life. I was absolutely astounded at what I saw. There was a consistent pattern that clearly demonstrated his love and involvement in directing my entire life.

Perhaps by reading the story of my life, you will be better able to recognize God's involvement in your life much sooner than I did.

The Author

Chapter One

The Early Years

Anyone familiar with the circumstances surrounding my birth and childhood would have said that the prospects for my future were rather bleak. They would have predicted that I would receive only a limited education and spend my entire life in an economic ghetto subsisting on welfare with the real possibility that I might end up in jail. I am an African-American born to an unwed mother. I had three or four half brothers and sisters, but the youngest of them was 17 years older than I. They had already left home or were about to do so when I was born, so I didn't get to know them during my childhood. It was just my mother and I living together in a tiny upstairs apartment. The good news is that God loves everyone regardless of the circumstances of their birth. With his help, everyone can rise above the very worst of circumstances. Life is a gift from God. What's important is not where or how your life began, but what you do with your life and how you finish it.

As you read about the various events in my life, keep asking yourself if those things happened by chance or if they were guided by God's unseen hand. I am confident that you will come to the same conclusion that I did—that there is something more at work in our lives than mere chance. Next, I want you to look for similar events in your life. Before long, you will see a pattern that makes it abundantly clear that a higher power is at work in your life. You can have no better guide than the one who made you, loves you, and knows you better than anyone else ever could. Your greatest fulfillment in life will come when you learn to recognize that guidance and follow it. Just be aware that your experiences will not be identical to mine. Just as no two people are the same, even so, everyone's experiences are different. God will uniquely design your experiences to suit your personality.

As evidence that God provides personalized guidance in our lives, he says the following in Isaiah 48:17: "I am the Lord your God, who teaches you to profit, who leads you in the way you should go" (RSV). That promise has been fulfilled numerous times in my life, and it is available to everyone.

I have some surprisingly vivid memories of the first two years of my life. One of the fondest of those memories is a little red wagon that my mother bought for me. I loved that wagon! My mother used to load it up with empty milk bottles and send me off to the store down the street to buy more milk. Somehow I managed to accomplish the task even at that young age.

Another memory of that time was the day a man came to the apartment. I can still see him sitting at the kitchen table conversing with my mother. She brought me to him and said, "Oscar, this is your father." If my memory serves me correctly, I believe she said his name was William Daniels. He left a short time after the introductions were made, and I never saw him again.

A few weeks or months later, my mother stepped outside the front door and onto the landing at the top of the stairs and let out a frightening and gut-wrenching scream. As a two-year-old child, I had no idea what was happening, but when I look back on that moment now, I'm sure she was having a nervous breakdown. Apparently, the pressures of being a single mother had gotten to be too much for her. The next thing I knew, I was taken by the authorities and placed in an orphanage in the city of Pittsburgh, Pennsylvania. For some reason, I still remember the address of that orphanage. It was located at 3333 Forbes Street.

I spent the next two years of my life at the orphanage. I must have had quite a sassy mouth even at that early age. Something I said so offended or shocked one of the staff members that she grabbed a bar of Octagon laundry soap and washed my mouth out with it. To this day, I have no idea what I could have said that would have warranted such a harsh reaction.

My other memories of the orphanage are much more pleasant. I remember being in bed at night and watching lights from passing cars shine on the ceiling briefly and disappear one after the other until I fell asleep.

One of my favorite places at the orphanage was the playground out back. It had all the typical playground equipment that was available in those days, including seesaws, sliding boards, monkey bars, and a sandbox, and I spent many happy moments there playing with the other orphans. The playground had a brick wall around it that was about four feet tall. I noticed that numerous adults would pause at the wall to watch us play. I didn't pay much attention to them, and I assumed that they were just passersby who were momentarily attracted by the laughter and activities of the children. It turns out, however, that they were prospective foster parents who were trying to decide which of the children they would take into their homes. I was fortunate to be chosen by Ulysses and Louise Williams when I was four years old. Was it a mere chance occurrence that they chose me, or was it divine intervention? Read the rest of my story and see what conclusion you reach.

Mr. Williams was a dentist with his own private practice, and I believe his wife was college educated. They lived in a beautiful brick house with their own four children by birth. There was Elinor, who was three years older than I and who became my big sister. Another daughter was Ruth, who was already a schoolteacher. A son whose name escapes me was in college busily preparing for a professional career. I believe but am not certain that his name was Leon. Ulysses Jr. was the other sibling in the family, and he later got drafted into the army during World War II. So, in just four short years, I went from living in the ghetto to living in an upper middle-class home. At that time, I was not aware of the significance of those events, but I now look back on them as major evidence of God's direct involvement in my life at a very early age.

Living with the Williams family was one of the best things that could have happened to me at that point in my life. They were a warm and loving family, and through them, God provided a wonderful environment for me. With her skills as a teacher, Ruth taught me how to read before I was old enough to go to school. I became a lifelong avid reader, and that put me far ahead of my classmates in elementary school. It also enabled me to skip one of the early grades in school.

The Williams family were devout Christians, and every Sunday they went to Central Baptist Church located at the corner of Wylie Avenue and Soho Street. Cornell Talley was the minister at the church. Pastor Talley was eloquent and persuasive, and he had a wonderful personality. He was greatly loved and admired by the entire congregation. Even at my young age, I thoroughly enjoyed every aspect of the services including children's Sunday school, vacation Bible school in the summer, and the main worship service with the adults. One feature of the church service that I enjoyed the most was when, dressed in splendid robes, the choir marched down the center aisle to take their seats in the choir loft at the front of the church. As they marched, the organ played at maximum volume, and the choir loudly and joyfully sang the following words: "Holy, holy, holy, Lord God almighty. Early in the morning, our song shall rise to thee …" It was an awe-inspiring moment at the start of every church service, and it had a profound impact on me.

It was in Sunday school and in the Williams household that I learned numerous Bible verses and hymns. It was there that I learned to pray and learned the moral values that have served me so well throughout my life. The Williams family could have given me no better gift than that. They enriched my young life in so many ways that my birth mother would not have been able to do even though she loved me very much.

God's hand was upon me way back then as it has been all throughout my life. His hand is upon you, too, and you can find the guidance if you will only look for it.

Life with the Williams family was idyllic. I had an abundance of toys and good food, but most importantly, I received genuine love and acceptance. Then something unexpected happened that I now believe was divinely ordained.

When the Williams family took me into their home, they were fully prepared to keep me until I was grown. However, something happened that resulted in my leaving that home when I was eight years old. As my life's story unfolds before you, it will become evident that God's hand was involved in that unexpected turn of events. Mr. and Mrs. Williams were going away on a two-week vacation or cruise, and they couldn't take me with them. They asked the orphanage that was responsible for my care to temporarily place me in another foster home until they came back. The home they chose for me was that of Mr. and Mrs. Mason at 2510 Hallett Street (I don't remember their first names). Mr. Mason was a barber, and I believe he had his own shop on Fulton Street. Mrs. Mason was a loving housewife who managed her household well. We called them Mama Mason and Papa Mason. The home had two other foster boys around my age (Clifford Pinno and George Nixon). The home also had a dog, which was something I had never had before. I had such a wonderful time in that home during those two weeks that I did something that would completely alter my entire future.

As planned, I returned to the Williams household when they came back from their vacation. However, when school was over every day, I went to the Mason household to play with the boys and the dog. The first time I did that, the Williams family had no idea where I was until I showed up at their house just before dark. When this happened day after day, they concluded that I might be happier living with the Mason family. With my happiness in mind, they asked the orphanage to see if the Masons would be willing to take me into their home permanently. The Masons agreed, and I was transferred to their home. At age eight, I was too young to realize what I was losing when I left the Williams household, but I was happy living with the Masons. God knew that the future he had planned for me would be better served if I lived with the Masons.

Clifford was an extremely gifted young boy who was skilled at working with wood. I have no idea how he acquired those skills at such a young age. They just seemed to come naturally to him, and I learned a great deal from him that has served me well throughout my life. I believe it was he who built the doghouse in our backyard. For another project, he found some narrow planks of wood that had been discarded. They were about six feet long and were perfect for what he had in mind. He cut blocks of wood from a 2x4 and nailed one block to each plank to create a pair of stilts for each of the boys. We had a great deal of fun walking around the neighborhood on stilts as if we were six feet tall.

Clifford also built go-carts for us similar to those used in a soapbox derby. He scoured the neighborhood and scrounged up the lumber, axle rods, and wheels from discarded baby carriages or other sources. Hallett Street was located on a hill, and we thoroughly enjoyed riding our carts down the hill. Clifford was a natural-born genius, and I learned so much from him. I'm not sure what he ended up doing in life, but he would have been a great engineer, architect, or building contractor.

Those were simpler and safer times when I moved in with the Mason family around 1944, and it was generally safe for me to play and go anywhere in the city. Child abductions or molestations were practically unheard of. In that environment, Mrs. Mason would send us out to play after we did our chores, and she had no idea where we were. We always showed up at mealtimes and at bedtime, and Mrs. Mason had perfect peace of mind concerning us. Those were truly carefree times. We played hide-and-seek and cops and robbers with our cap guns and water pistols. When we played cowboys and Indians, a broomstick between our legs served as a horse. We played marbles, went roller skating, jumped rope, and played hopscotch. Some of us had BB guns and practiced shooting at tin cans and sometimes at each other. These activities were great fun, but they were not enough for me. I was a very adventurous boy, and I often wandered off alone for miles outside of the neighborhood to explore various parts of the city.

One of the places I discovered was a YMCA about a mile from home. I found out that it had a swimming pool, and when I saw all of the children having so much fun in the pool, I decided that I wanted to go swimming, even though I had never done so before. Since this was my first time in a pool, I was unaware that there was a deep end and a shallow end of the pool. Unfortunately, I jumped into the deep end and immediately began to sink under the water. Frantically I kicked and clawed my way to the top of the water and screamed for help. There was a young man nearby who heard my screams. In an instant he was at my side. He put his arm around me and got me over to the edge of the pool. Working through that young man, God rescued me and saved my life. Were it not for the grace of God, my life could have ended before it really got started. I no longer view things like that as "just a lucky break."

For some reason, that experience did not give me a fear of water. I walked down to the shallow end of the pool where I could clearly see that the other children were able to stand on the bottom with their heads and torsos out of the water. I practiced putting my head under the water while holding my breath. Then I taught myself to push off and float on the surface of the water. Then while floating, I began to kick my feet in the water and to use my arms to pull myself forward. Within just one hour, I had gone from almost drowning to being a competent swimmer who felt perfectly comfortable in the water.

My love for swimming was so great that I acquired a pair of swimming trunks and went swimming three times a day in the summertime. I went to the pool at the YMCA in the morning and to another pool on Soho Street in the afternoon. In the evening, I went to a pool on Bedford Avenue that was open for night swimming. Those pools were in different parts of the city and miles away from where I lived. During the summer, I walked those long miles to the pools every day (Monday through Friday) without even noticing it. Those were some of the happiest days of my childhood.

A fourth foster boy was added to the Mason household. His name was John Polk. He blended nicely into the family and added a whole new dimension and set of experiences to our lives.

I am convinced that the Lord sent me to the Mason household in order to give me a very valuable gift, one that would serve me well all of my life. It was in that home that I developed a strong work ethic. Mrs. Mason gave us boys numerous chores to do, some of which had to be done every day and others that had to be done weekly or as needed. Some of the duties we had to perform without fail included dusting and polishing the furniture, sweeping and mopping the floors, vacuuming the carpets, washing and drying the dishes (there were no automatic dishwashers in those days), feeding and cleaning up after the pets, and running errands to the store and other places. Back in those days, houses were heated with coal-burning furnaces. Once or twice a year, the coal man would drop a truckload of coal in front of the house. We boys had to fill one wheelbarrow load after another, cart the coal to a basement window, and dump the coal onto a chute that carried it into the coal bin in the basement. It was hard work, and it took at least half a day or more to get all of the coal into the basement. Then we had to hose down the street to remove all of the coal dust residue. Each time coal was burned in the furnace, we also had to remove and safely dispose of the ashes (sometimes the ashes contained hot coals). I don't think I ever heard the boys complain about the work. It was good for us, and I think we actually enjoyed it.

One other responsibility we had was to hang clothes from the washing machine on the clothesline to dry. (In those days we didn't have clothes dryers.) The wet clothes had to be inserted between two revolving rollers to wring out as much water as possible before the clothes were ready to go on the clothesline. One day I was alone in the basement when my fingertip got caught between the rollers and my hand was pulled in. I began to yell and scream as the rollers pulled me in as far as my elbow. It pulled me in so far that I almost had to climb on top of the washing machine. By that time I was in full panic mode. Mrs. Mason came racing down, and by the time she got there, I was in almost up to my armpit. She had the presence of mind to pull the plug from the wall socket to stop the rollers from turning. Next, she hit the release mechanism to open up the rollers. If she had been a few seconds later, my arm might have been pulled from its socket. Needless to say, I was one relieved little boy.

As humans, we always want to be in full control of our circumstances, but God often guides us by circumstances that are beyond our control. Instead of being stressed about it when that happens, the best thing that we can do is to trust that God is in control and will make things turn out for our good. If you've been following my story closely thus far, you have already seen evidence of that principle at work in my life. As my story unfolds, you will see even more dramatic evidence of that principle at work in my life over and over again, and I hope that it will prompt you to look for similar evidence in your life.

God does not let go of our hand when circumstances are beyond our control. If anything, he grips it more securely. During a storm on the Sea of Galilee, Jesus was asleep at the back of the boat. The storm became so violent that the disciples feared for their lives. In total panic, they woke the Savior to apprise him of the danger. Jesus calmed the sea and stopped the wind from blowing. Then he rebuked the disciples for their lack of faith. He was trying to teach them that no matter how stormy life may get, God is still in control. The Bible says of God, "You will keep him in perfect peace whose mind is fixed on you because he trusts in you" (Isaiah 26:3). There is no greater peace that one can have than that which comes from complete faith and trust in God.

After I had been in the Mason household for four years, we got the sad news that Mrs. Mason had stomach cancer and would no longer be able to take care of us. The boys were separated, and we all went to different foster homes. I went to a large two-story apartment at 2338 Webster Avenue. The lady who was to be my new foster mother was Mattie Parham. She was an older woman who was either a widow or a divorcee. The apartment was huge and had many bedrooms, one of which she rented to an older male relative of hers named Tanner Johnson. Mr. Johnson worked at one of the many steel mills in the Pittsburgh area. At the time, she had one other foster child named Ralph Jackson, although she would later take in three more. One of those three boys suffered from gender confusion and turned out to be a flamboyant transvestite. He loved to parade around the neighborhood wearing lipstick, high-heeled shoes, and women's dresses. Needless to say, he was the talk of the neighborhood.

Mrs. Parham was a very industrious woman. In addition to the money she got from renting a room and taking in foster children, she also took in laundry, all of which I believe she did on an old-fashioned scrub board. She had a couple of well-to-do clients who brought their clothes to her for laundering. She took great pride in her work, carefully starching and ironing the men's dress shirts. The clients were always pleased with her work and her dependability.

I remember one occasion when she accidentally scorched one of the shirts she was ironing. She was practically in tears, and I think she was a bit terrified that she would lose a customer. Of course she was forgiven, with no loss of customer loyalty.

In the neighborhood where I now lived, there was a somewhat eccentric young man who was a pigeon fancier who built an eight square-foot pigeon coop in a nearby field. Scores of pigeons nested in the coop every night and ate the food he provided. It was thrilling to watch whole flocks of pigeons fly out of the coop at one time and then return periodically throughout the day. I learned a lot from that man—not so much about pigeons, but how he constructed the coop. I learned how to anchor the foundation so the structure would not move when wind or rainstorms beat against it. I learned how to put up the frame, leaving space for the doorway and windows, hang the door on hinges, and attach the wallboards to the frame. I learned how to cover the outside with tarpaper to keep the rain out. We boys in the neighborhood imitated what he had done by building our own clubhouse next to the pigeon coop. It was quite an education for a boy such as I who was still in his early teens. The things I learned there would serve me well throughout my life. God knew I would need those skills later, and in a rather unusual way he provided them to me at this particular point in my life. The things we experience day by day are building blocks that are clearly designed to prepare us for that which is to come in the future. It's difficult to see it when it's happening, but when you look back over your entire life, you can clearly see the pattern.

Every Sunday, Mrs. Parham took us to Macedonia Baptist Church on Bedford Avenue. Unlike the much more sedate congregation at Central Baptist Church, the congregation at Macedonia was more exuberant and expressive. There was a lot of very rhythmic gospel music, and there was likely to be a lot of people who would break out in joyous shouting whenever the music moved them or the preaching reached a fevered pitch. It was not uncommon to see a lot of ladies and a few men shouting joyfully while dancing up and down the aisle with their arms raised over their heads. It was different from anything I had ever seen before. Even though it was not something I could imagine myself doing, the gospel music and stirring sermons still satisfied a need I had and helped to keep me exposed to the gospel message.

My birth mother was now well enough to locate me, and she came to visit me at Mrs. Parham's home. We had been separated so long that she was like a stranger to me. I was glad to see her, but I don't think I felt any special bond with her. She brought me some nice gifts that I was delighted to receive. We visited for a few hours and then she left. I never saw her again. She made no effort to regain custody of me. I believe she felt that I would be better off where I was than with her. As my story unfolds, you will see that she was right. I had to be where I was for purposes known only to God at the time. My life would have been dramatically different if she had taken me away. Years later, I learned from a cousin that my mother died of stomach cancer at age 55. By my calculation, that would have been a year or two after our visit.

One of my half brothers also located me at Mrs. Parham's home and came to visit me. I don't recall his real name. He was called "Red" because of his reddish-brown hair. He had been working in a garage some years before, and the garage door came down on his legs. Both legs had to be amputated below the knees. He was fitted with artificial legs and was able to walk without crutches or a cane, and he could also drive a car. During my conversation with him, I learned that he led a pretty wild life that included chasing women, drinking, and gambling. He invited me to come and live with him, suggesting that I could participate in those activities as well. I thank God that I said no. I learned later that he accidentally killed himself while playing Russian roulette. There is no telling what would have happened to me if I had gone with him. The only thing I know for certain is that nothing good would have come from it.

During my early teen years while I was living in Mrs. Parham's home, I went through a slump at school. Not only was I getting failing grades, but I was constantly getting into trouble. On at least three or four occasions, Mrs. Parham was called to the school to discuss the matter with the principal. After one such meeting, she was in the kitchen discussing the matter with her tenant, Mr. Johnson. They were unaware that I was in the next room and could hear everything they said. Mrs. Parham was explaining the situation to Mr. Johnson. In exasperation, she concluded her remarks by saying, "I just don't know what to do about Oscar." Then I heard Mr. Johnson say, "Aw, that boy will never amount to anything."

The Lord knew that I needed to hear those words, and I have no doubt that he arranged for me to do so. At the time, I wasn't consciously aware of what God was doing in my life, but when I look back upon it, I can see it oh so clearly. I didn't consciously say to myself that I would show him, but apparently at some subconscious level, those words from Mr. Johnson both sobered me and galvanized me. I immediately went from all failing grades to straight "A's" with an occasional "B" thrown in. I maintained those high grades all the way through junior and senior high school. Years later, I graduated with honors and have maintained those high academic standards ever since. Thank you, Lord, for that kick in the pants just when I needed it most.

My Spiritual Growth Reaches a Whole New Level of Maturity

While living at Mrs. Parham's, several seminal events occurred that profoundly changed and affected the rest of my life. During that time, I read a lot of comic books. In the back of many of them there were various advertisements. One recurring ad was one for a muscle-building course by Charles Atlas. I desperately wanted to have the course so I could have rock-hard abs and big bulging muscles like he did, but I didn't have the money to pay for it. There was a grocery store in the neighborhood owned by a Jewish couple, Joseph and Shirley Landau. What was so unusual about them was the fact that they were very strict about eating only kosher meats at home, but in the store, they sold and ate pork and all kinds of non-kosher meats. I never could figure out how that made any sense to them. In spite of that inconsistency in the practice of their faith, they were really nice people. I approached Mr. Landau and asked him if I could work at his store to earn the money I needed. He said he didn't really need any help, but he hired me anyway. He put me to work stocking shelves, making deliveries, and keeping the store clean. In short order I had the money I needed. This was the first of many instances when I needed or wanted something and God immediately provided the means to obtain it.

Something else happened that had an impact on my life in a very profound way. Ruth Williams had taught me how to read when I was only four years old and had bestowed upon me a great love for books. By now, I was a voracious reader. Not a day went by that I wasn't reading a book or magazine. As soon as I finished one book, I would start another. One book that I found in Mrs. Parham's home was one that told the story of prominent people who are mentioned in the Bible. There were such people as Abraham, Isaac, Jacob, Moses, King David, Daniel, and others. Unfortunately, I don't remember the name of the book, but it was while reading it that I had a spiritual awakening in my soul. I knew beyond all doubt that what I was reading was true. I knew that God was real and that he is involved in the lives of men and women. I began a quest to know him, to know about his dealings with people, and to know his will for our lives.

Ever since that time, I read a portion of the Bible every day. What better way is there to learn about God than by reading the book he inspired and that quotes him directly? Over the course of my life, I have read the Bible all the way through many times. I find it to be a great source of comfort, inspiration, wisdom, moral values, and guidance for all aspects of my life. Most importantly, it revealed more to me about God and showed how he expects me to conduct my life. It shows me what God will do for me in this life and what glories await me in the afterlife. The Bible has done more to influence my life and my thinking than any other book. I am eternally grateful that God preserved it for more than three thousand years and made it so readily available today for all those who wish to know him.

Around that time, I kept seeing classified ads in the magazines and comic books I was reading. The ads were placed by an organization called Life Study Fellowship. I was intrigued by their ads, and so I requested the literature they were offering. In that material, they explained how to give one's life to God. I followed their instructions by kneeling before God and raising my hands toward heaven. I said the short prayer they suggested and surrendered my life to God. That was merely the first step in my walk with God. My journey had just begun, and many wonderful adventures lay ahead.

About a block away from where I lived, there was a small storefront attached to one of the nicer homes in our neighborhood. Inside the storefront was a convenience store owned by Mr. Goodman, a prosperous African-American businessman. Years earlier, I used to go into the store and slip candy bars into my pocket and then leave without paying for them. After my spiritual awakening, I was impressed to confess to Mr. Goodman what I had done and to make restitution. In those days, candy bars sold for five or ten cents or for a quarter at the most. With enough money to pay for twenty or so candy bars, I approached Mr. Goodman, made my confession, and gave him the money. Mr. Goodman was so impressed that he excitedly called to his wife to come into the store from the house. When he told her what I had done, she smiled approvingly and gave me the nicest compliment. I left the store with a sense of relief and the satisfaction of knowing that I had done the right thing.

The Goodmans' daughter reacted to me in a different way than her parents did. When she saw me in the neighborhood sometime later, I was standing with my back against the wall of a building. She came over to me, pressed her body close to mine, and very seductively told me that I could have anything I wanted. Fortunately, I was too young and too naïve to know what it was that I was supposed to want. Already, Satan was trying to lure me from the path I had chosen.

When I was growing up, evangelists used to pitch large tents on vacant lots in various places in the city and conduct evangelistic meetings in an effort to win converts to Christ and the church. In 1953, when I was sixteen, I noticed a flyer in our mailbox announcing an upcoming series of evangelistic meetings that were going to be held in an open field several blocks from our apartment. The topics of the sermons that were going to be preached during the first week of meetings intrigued me, and I decided I would go. I put the flyer on my desk so I would be reminded of the meetings when the time came to go. When I later looked for the flyer, it was missing. I asked Mrs. Parham if she had seen it. She said she thought it was just some junk mail and had thrown it away. Determined to find it, I searched through the garbage piece by piece until I found it.

On opening night, I found my way to the big tent. The tent was enormous. Inside, the ground was covered with sawdust, and hundreds of folding chairs were arranged in two sections to create a center aisle between the sections. The platform was beautifully decorated and had a choir loft behind the podium and a piano on the far left side. I believe there was an organ on the right side, but I'm less certain about that.

I slipped into the tent and took a seat among the hundreds of other people who were there. A song leader led us in singing some gospel hymns. When the time came for the meeting to begin, the pianist began to play the following song as the audience sang along softly and meditatively:

> Turn your eyes upon Jesus,
>
> Look full in his wonderful face,
>
> And the things of earth will grow strangely dim
>
> In the light of his glory and grace.

That song had such a sweet melody and such a powerful message that sixty years after I first heard it, I am still moved by it every time I hear it, and it takes me back in memory to that tent meeting all those years ago.

As that song was softly sung, the ministers walked reverently onto the platform, knelt briefly for a moment of silent prayer, and then stood up to take their seats. After a few preliminary remarks and announcements were made, the evangelist, Leon Cox, stood up to preach. He was dynamic and eloquent, but more than that, his message had substance and was biblically accurate. I could agree with everything he said. I was so moved by the message that I went every night throughout the summer. I was growing spiritually and increasing in knowledge with every sermon. Near the end of the campaign, the evangelist made an appeal for people to come forward if they wanted to join the church. By then, I was in complete agreement with all of his sermons and the doctrines of the church. I got up and went to the front to join the others who had also gone forward. This was a major milestone and turning point in my life. I didn't know it then, but so much of my future hung on that one decision. That decision determined the college I attended, the career I pursued, the person I married, and so much more.

Some Basic Bible Doctrines Seen in a Whole New Light-- the Light of God's Word and History

The church I had joined was the Seventh-day Adventist Church. Who are Seventh-day Adventists? As the name implies, they are Christians who observe the seventh day of the week (Saturday) as their Sabbath day and who are looking forward to the second advent or coming of Jesus Christ. However, we are much more than just our name. First of all, we believe that the entire Bible is the inspired word of God, and we are committed to living in harmony with its teachings rather than by any doctrines of man. We eat only those things that the Bible says we may eat, and we abstain from those things that are forbidden. Among those things from which we abstain are alcoholic beverages, tobacco, narcotics, and certain specified kinds of meat and seafood that the Bible says we should not eat because they are unclean. As a result of our strict adherence to those principles, scientific studies show that Adventists live longer and have far fewer diseases than the general population.

Which Day is the Sabbath Day Chosen by God, and Did He Ever Change It?

Why do Seventh-day Adventists observe Saturday as the Sabbath day? They do that because God designated that day as a day of rest and worship, and he never changed it. To make sure that there was no doubt about which day was the Sabbath, God rained down manna for the children of Israel to eat. Every day from Sunday to Thursday, he rained down just enough for one day. They were to go out on each of those days and collect enough for that particular day. They were not to keep any of it overnight (if they did, it would spoil). On

Friday, however, God rained down extra manna, and they were to collect double the usual amount on that day. They were to eat half of it on Friday and keep the other half overnight to eat the next day (this time, the manna that was kept overnight did not spoil). This was done so they would not have to go out and collect manna on the Sabbath day. No manna fell from heaven on the Sabbath day. God repeated this over and over again for 40 long years. By doing this, he clearly showed them which day he had designated as the Sabbath day. Because of that 40-year-long demonstration, there could be no doubt in anyone's mind about which day was the Sabbath day. Jesus, his disciples, the apostles, and the early church all observed Saturday as the Sabbath day. The change from Saturday to Sunday was made by man long after the apostles were dead and gone, but it was made without authorization by God.

If Saturday is the true Sabbath day, why do so many people observe Sunday? Many reasons are given for that practice, none of which are valid:

Reason Number One

They do it in honor of the resurrection, which was on a Sunday.

Response

That's a nice sentiment, but it was not authorized by God or by Jesus. Even after the resurrection, Jesus, his disciples, and the early church continued to observe Saturday as the Sabbath day. God intended for the Sabbath day to be a permanent memorial to the work he did in creating the world. That's why he put it at the end of the week after he had done his work instead of at the beginning of the week before he had started to work. It was to be a recurring reminder that he is our maker, provider, and the source of everything that exists. To demonstrate the permanence of the seventh day as the Sabbath, he engraved it in stone in the Ten Commandments. There is nothing in the Bible to suggest that he ever changed it. Later in this book, I will show from historical documents that it was man who changed it, and not God. I will show you who did it, why it was done, and when it was done. I will also show that those who made one change did so on their own initiative without being authorized by God or the Bible. It's in the historical records for all to see.

Reason Number Two

It doesn't matter what day you keep holy as long as you pick one.

Response

This is one of the worst possible reasons of all. It implies that God doesn't really mean what he says. That's the very same lie that Satan told Eve when he tempted her to eat the forbidden fruit, and that same lie is being told today in regard to the Sabbath commandment. People who say that we can keep holy any day we wish are essentially saying that what God wants doesn't matter. The Ten Commandments are not ten suggestions or guidelines. They are ten requirements. God does not issue vague commandments and then make some of them optional. It is illogical to say that we must strictly obey some of the commandments (thou shalt not kill, steal, commit adultery, etc.), but the Sabbath commandment is optional. One of the very first lessons that Adam and Eve learned in the Garden of Eden was that God means exactly what he says.

Reason Number Three

Paul said that we are under grace and not under the law.

Response

Paul also said that being under grace does not mean that we can disregard the law or disobey it. In Romans 3:31, Paul says, "Do we then make void the law through faith? God forbid! Yea, we establish the law." Nowhere does Paul say that being under grace eliminates the need to obey the Ten Commandments. When he says that we are under grace, he was merely trying to emphasize the fact that salvation comes through Christ alone. There is nothing we can do to earn it.

Reason Number Four

The apostle Paul says, "Let no man judge you concerning sabbath days" (Colossians 2:16).

Response

If you look closely at the text in Colossians 2:16, Paul makes it abundantly clear that he is not talking about the weekly Sabbath day. You will notice that the word he uses is "sabbath days" (plural) and not "the Sabbath day" (singular). There were many festival sabbaths (days of rest and celebration) throughout the year, but there was only one Sabbath that occurred every week and is embedded right in the middle of the Ten Commandment law. Paul was probably referring to the annual sabbath celebrations written by Moses. He was not referring to the Ten Commandment law, which was personally written by God and engraved in stone. Paul would never tell anyone to disregard the Ten Commandments. The weekly Sabbath was regularly observed by Paul and the apostles.

Reason Number Five

Sunday was good enough for my parents and grandparents, so it's good enough for me.

Response

God forgives those who don't know the truth, but he says in James 4:17 that it is a sin for the person who knows to do right and doesn't do it. God does not overlook deliberate disobedience.

Reason Number Six

The apostle Paul told the believers at one location to assemble themselves together on the first day of the week.

Response

Many people interpret that text to mean that the Sabbath had been changed from Saturday to Sunday, but that is not true. Paul told them to assemble on the first day of the week for the purpose of gathering funds to finance his ministry and also to discuss other business such as providing support for poor churches in other locations. They no doubt felt that these matters were inappropriate to deal with on the Sabbath day, so they came together on the first day of the week for those purposes. Nothing in the text implies that the Sabbath had been changed.

As we see from reading 2 Corinthians 9, Paul's custom was to send people to a city ahead of his arrival so funds for the support of his work and of the poor could be gathered ahead of time. It was an efficient way to handle those matters, and it had nothing to do with worshipping on the first day of the week. That day was designated primarily for the purposes of gathering funds.

For Paul, it was also a matter of scheduling the fundraising effort ahead of his arrival so that it would not have to be done hurriedly after he arrived. It had nothing to do with worship or observance of the Sabbath day on Sunday, the first day of the week. The Sabbath didn't get changed to Sunday until three hundred years after Paul's time. A little bit later in this chapter, I will reveal exactly when and by whom it was changed.

Reason Number Seven

Hundreds of millions of Christians observe Sunday as their sabbath day. That many people can't all be wrong, can they?

Response

Sure, they can all be wrong. Jesus says that "wide is the gate, and broad is the way, that leadeth to destruction, and many there be which go in thereat; because strait is the gate, and narrow is the way, which leadeth unto life, and few there be that find it"

(Matthew 7:13, 14). He also says that many are called, but few are chosen. When sin and corruption were so rampant in the earth that God destroyed the whole world with a flood, only eight people were saved on the ark (Noah and his family). When God rained down fire and brimstone to destroy Sodom and Gomorrah because of their widespread wickedness, only three people out of the thousands in those cities were spared (Lot and his two daughters). Even though millions of Israelites were freed from slavery and bondage in Egypt, only two out of that original group made it into the Promised Land (Joshua and Caleb)--all of the others who made it were the next generation of Israelites. Because of the original generation's murmuring, complaining, and disobedience, they all died in the wilderness and never made it into the Promised Land. Those examples show that being in the majority is no assurance of being right or of being saved. So it's never wise to simply follow the crowd. Will all of those people be lost, you may ask? Of course not. If their hearts are right with God and they are living right to the best of their knowledge, they will certainly be saved. The thief dying on the cross next to Jesus had probably not kept the commandments very well, but his conversion and faith in Jesus were enough for him to be saved. His heart had been changed. Those who come to Jesus must do so with hearts that are willing to do whatever God commands when it is revealed to them. If their hearts are so inclined, they can be saved. As Jesus says, "Man looks upon the outward appearance, but God looks upon the heart (1 Samuel 16:7). The wisest policy is to ask yourself what the Bible has to say on any given question and then align yourself with the word of God. The Bible is abundantly clear about which day God has designated as the Sabbath day. The only question is whether we will observe the day that God has chosen or the day that man has chosen.

Reason Number Eight

Some people quote part of a Bible text that says the commandments were nailed to the cross. Based on that text, they say we don't have to keep them anymore.

Response

The people who make that claim will acknowledge that it's wrong to kill, steal, lie, covet, and commit adultery, but it's interesting how they single out the Sabbath day as the one commandment that we don't have to keep. The people who use that text as a reason to disregard the Sabbath commandment fail to quote the entire text, which says that the things that were nailed to the cross were the commandments "contained in ordinances." (See Ephesians 2 and Colossians 2.) There are no ordinances in the Ten Commandments, so it is clear that Paul could not have been talking about that law. The Ten Commandments are very direct and to the point—it simply says "thou shalt" and "thou shalt not." There is not a single ordinance anywhere among them.

By contrast, the sacrificial and ceremonial laws are full of ordinances. They stipulate what kinds of animals are to be used for sacrifices, the manner in which they are to be sacrificed, what is to be done with the blood, what to do with the internal organs of the animals, what to do with the meat afterwards, and the list of ordinances goes on and on. It is those laws and not the Ten Commandments that were nailed to the cross.

The sacrificial or ceremonial laws were always intended to be temporary. They served two primary purposes: (1) to remind the people that sin is so abhorrent to God that it warrants death or it requires a blood sacrifice to atone for it, and (2) it served to point their minds forward to the one perfect and true sacrifice that would be made when Christ died on the cross. Once Christ died, those sacrificial laws were no longer necessary and were figuratively "nailed to the cross" with him.

We must continually make a clear distinction between the sacrificial or ceremonial laws and the Ten Commandment law. The former were dictated by God, and then Moses wrote them in a book or on a scroll. By contrast, the Ten Commandment law is the only law that God personally wrote with his own hand. To demonstrate its permanence, he engraved it in stone and preserved it in the ark. The seventh-day Sabbath is embedded right in the middle of the Ten Commandments. God intended for it to be a permanent reminder of the work he did when he created the world. He wanted to make sure that we didn't forget it or take it for granted. That's why the Sabbath was placed at the end of the workweek instead of the beginning, and it's also why the commandment begins with the word "remember." Below is a copy of the fourth commandment. Read it carefully and you will see what God was trying to accomplish by giving it to us as a weekly reminder of the work he did in creating the world:

> Remember the sabbath day to keep it holy. Six days shalt thou labor and do all thy work, but the seventh day is the sabbath of the Lord thy God. In it, thou shalt not do any work, thou nor thy son nor thy daughter, nor thy manservant, nor thy maidservant, nor thy cattle, nor the stranger that is within thy gates. For in six days the Lord made heaven and earth, the seas and all that is in them, and rested the seventh day. Wherefore, the Lord blessed the sabbath day and hallowed it.

God clearly intended for the Sabbath day to be a permanent reminder of creation.

To further demonstrate the permanence of the seventh-day Sabbath, the Bible says in Isaiah 66 that the Sabbath day will be observed in heaven and on the new earth throughout all eternity. It says that from one Sabbath to another and from one new moon to another shall all flesh come to worship before him. There will be no confusion in heaven about which day is the true Sabbath. It will be the same one that Jesus observed when he was on earth and the one he taught us to observe by his example. The Bible says that it was his custom to go into the synagogue on the Sabbath—the same Sabbath that the Jews observed since the

Ten Commandments were first given by God. Man's opinions about it won't be relevant. If we are going to observe the seventh day as the Sabbath in heaven and on the new earth, we might as well get started now and get used to it.

The psalmist David said, "All his [God's] commandments are sure. They stand fast for ever and ever" (Psalm 111:7 and 8). The sacrificial laws served a temporary purpose. When Christ died on the cross as the true and only effective sacrifice, the purpose of the sacrificial law was fulfilled, and now we no longer need to observe those laws, but as David said, the [ten] commandments are eternal and will be applicable forever.

In the Bible, God says of himself, "I am God, and I change not." Several centuries ago, people took it upon themselves to change the Sabbath day from Saturday to Sunday, but God never authorized it. Why would a perfect and unchanging God create a perfect law and then change it because some people thought they had a better idea? God is eternal, and so is his law (and that includes every part of it—not just nine-tenths of it).

As a further indication of the permanence of the Ten Commandments, Jesus said in Matthew 5 that he had not come to destroy the law, but to fulfill it. He went on to pronounce judgments upon those who broke the law and taught others to break it. There might be some question as to whether Jesus was referring to the sacrificial laws or the Ten Commandment law. He strictly adhered to both of them. He fulfilled the purpose of the sacrificial law by sacrificing himself for our sins, and he adhered strictly to the Ten Commandment law by his conduct and by going to the synagogue every Sabbath day to worship in observance of the fourth commandment. Jesus didn't come to destroy either law, and he condemns those who teach others to disregard either law. On another occasion, a rich young ruler came to Jesus and asked what he needed to do to inherit eternal life. Jesus told him to keep the commandments. To make it clear that he was talking about the Ten Commandments, Jesus recited a few of them.

Another time, the disciples asked Jesus how they could know in advance when he would be returning to the earth. Jesus gave them a long list of things to look for (see Matthew 24). He said there would first be a terrible time of trouble such as the world has never seen before. There would be wars and rumors of wars. There would also be widespread violent earthquakes, famines, pestilences, diseases, and death. Things will be so bad that people will have to flee from their homes in order to escape those horrible tragedies. Then Jesus said something very interesting. He said pray that your flight will not be in the winter or on the Sabbath. If the Sabbath day can be on Friday or Sunday or any other day we choose, then that statement by Jesus is meaningless. His statement only has meaning if he is referring to a specific day of the week, and the only day specified by God as a day of rest and worship is the seventh-day Sabbath. That statement by Jesus clearly indicates that he expects his followers to be keeping the Sabbath commandment right up to the very end of the world and beyond.

Jesus also said that only those who do the will of the Father in heaven will enter the kingdom of heaven. The Father's will for us certainly includes obedience to his commandments (not some of the commandments or most of the commandments, but all of them). I would take seriously what Jesus says on this matter. There is no greater authority on this subject than he.

In the book of Revelation, the apostle John was given a guided tour of heaven and was shown glimpses of the future. At one point, the angel shows John those who are candidates for the kingdom of heaven. He describes them as those who keep the commandments and have the faith of Jesus (Revelation 14:12).

The angel does not say that the ones who will enter heaven are the ones who keep nine-tenths of the commandments or most of the commandments. The clear implication is that the ones who will enter the kingdom of heaven are the ones who keep all of the commandments. They are the ones who put God first in their lives. They are the ones who put obedience to God above their own desires and above their own private interpretation of the commandments. As John is beholding the splendor of heaven, he hears the voice of Jesus saying, "Blessed are they that do his commandments, that they may have right to the tree of life, and may enter in through the gates into the city [of heaven]" (Revelation 22:14).

If, as these texts indicate, the only ones going into heaven are those who have kept the commandments, it suggests that the commandments are critically important and should not be taken lightly. I would be leery of anyone who teaches that the commandments were abolished and that we no longer have to keep them. That kind of false doctrine contradicts the teachings of Jesus and can have eternal consequences for the people who believe it.

Bible-believing Christians know that the only way to get to heaven is by accepting the atoning sacrifice of Jesus Christ. We cannot get to heaven by keeping the commandments or by any effort on our part. We don't keep the commandments in order to be saved. We keep them because we have been saved, because Jesus commands us to do so, and because we eagerly obey whatever our Savior commands us to do.

When and by Whom was the Sabbath Day Changed from Saturday to Sunday?

If God did not change the Sabbath commandment, then who did change it? The Catholic Church is the principal organization that changed the Sabbath day from Saturday to Sunday, and virtually every other Christian church has followed its lead. Roman Emperor Constantine had apparently been a sun worshipper before his conversion to Christianity and, of course, his day of worship would have been Sunday. At the time of his conversion, the Church of Rome was still observing the seventh-day Sabbath of the Bible, but Constantine wanted the church to change the day of worship to Sunday so he could continue to worship on that day. Perhaps he was not fully converted and wanted to hedge his bets by appeasing both the sun god and the God of Christianity. As we learned from Paul's discourse with the Greeks on Mars Hill, it was not uncommon in those days for people to worship more than one god. There are some scholars who say that Constantine was not truly converted to Christianity at all, and that he simply wanted to unite his empire by blending the three major religions of his day: Judaism, Christianity, and Paganism. Since Jews and Christians were in the minority, it was easier to make them convert to Sunday worship. The Jews never converted, but the Catholics did. Although we can't be certain about Constantine's motives, we do know that in AD 321, Pope Sylvester I changed the biblical day of rest and worship from Saturday to Sunday.[1] At the Council of Laodicea in the fourth century AD, the Catholic Church made Sunday their official day of worship, and they specifically forbade their members from observing the so-called "Jewish Sabbath."[2] The Catholic Church has on numerous occasions acknowledged that they are the ones that changed the Sabbath day from Saturday to Sunday. On one such occasion, James Cardinal Gibbons wrote a treatise entitled *The Claims of the Catholic Church*.[3] In that treatise, he said the following: "The Divine institution of a day of rest from ordinary occupations and of religious worship, transferred by the authority of the Church from the Sabbath, the last day, to Sunday, the first day of the week, … is one of the most patent signs that we are a Christian people."

The Catholic Church was the dominant Christian religion for many centuries. As time went by, people soon forgot that Saturday is the true Sabbath day. When the Protestants pulled away from the Catholic Church during the reformation, they took the Sunday tradition with them. By that time, Sunday was the only Sabbath that they had ever known. That is how Sunday worship was perpetuated and disseminated throughout all of Christendom. So now we know that it was the Catholic Church that instituted the practice of Sunday worship and that they did it without being authorized by God to do so. So the question that we need to ask ourselves is whether we should obey God or man. The apostle Peter answered that question boldly and without hesitation when he said that we ought to obey God rather than man. I am in full agreement with him.

In Daniel 7:25, the Bible says that they shall think to change the times and laws. The things that the Catholic Church has done in regard to changing the Sabbath day seem to be a direct fulfillment of that prophecy. Read the endnotes at the back of the book for more information on how the Sabbath day was changed from Saturday to Sunday. You will be astounded at the hubris of those who took it upon themselves to make those changes in God's law.

As we have seen on the previous pages of this book, people give many different reasons for worshipping on Sunday. However, the action taken by the Catholic Church in changing the Sabbath day from Saturday to Sunday is the true reason why people worship on Sunday regardless of the various reasons they give in order to justify the practice. Without knowing it, millions of Christians are obeying the doctrines of men rather than the commandments of God.

Artist: Robert Eldridge. Used by permission of the Review and Herald Publishing Association.

The Ten Commandments

Can we pick and choose which ones to obey, or does God expect us to obey all of them?

The first line of the fourth commandment says, "Remember the sabbath day to keep it holy." Pastor Cox had a sermon entitled "What God Said Remember, and the Whole World Forgot." Most of the world has indeed forgotten the true Sabbath day. The last line of the fourth commandment says that God blessed and hallowed the seventh day of the week. However, many people choose various other days of the week as their day of worship. No matter how hard man tries, he cannot bless and hallow a day of his own choosing while ignoring the day that God has designated as the Sabbath. Only God can make a day hallowed or blessed, and he chose the seventh day, which came at the end of creation week. The Sabbath day is a memorial of creation week and is a constant reminder that the world and everything in it was made by God. As for me and my house, we're going with the Lord's choice.

What Happens to Us When We Die?

Another area where the Adventist Church is different from most other churches is on the question of what happens to people when they die. Many churches teach that you go immediately to heaven or hell depending on how you lived your life. It consoles people and makes them feel better to think that their deceased relatives and friends are up in heaven, but that's not what the Bible teaches. Jesus is the best authority on what happens to people when they die. He says that the hour is coming when all who are in the grave shall hear his voice and shall come forth (John 5:25–29). Since Jesus says they are in their graves waiting to be called forth, which means that they didn't go to heaven when they died. The apostle Paul affirms what Jesus had to say about where the dead are. He says that he doesn't want us to be ignorant about those who are "asleep." He goes on to say that when Jesus returns, he will descend from heaven with a shout, with the voice of an archangel and the trumpet of God, and the dead in Christ shall rise first (1 Thessalonians 4:16 and 17). If the dead are already in heaven as some Christians believe, there would be no need for the resurrection of which Jesus and Paul spoke.

In 1 Corinthians 15:51–53, the apostle Paul describes death as a kind of sleep from which we will be awakened at the resurrection. At that time, we will be given immortality and incorruptibility. That statement by Paul accords with what Jesus had to say about us being called forth from our graves at the resurrection. That makes much more sense than the idea that we first go to heaven and are then brought back to earth, put into our mortal bodies again so we can then be resurrected, made immortal, and then taken back to heaven. There are some who teach that idea, but there is no biblical authority for it.

Another popular misconception is that the human soul is immortal. It is one of the oldest lies ever told, and it has its origins way back in the Garden of Eden. Satan told Eve that she would not really die even though God had told her that she would if she ate the forbidden fruit. It is a falsehood that is in direct contradiction with everything that the Bible has to say on the subject. In Ezekiel 18:20, the Bible says that the soul that sins shall die. If the soul were truly immortal, it could not die no matter how sinful it was, but God says that it will die. Adam was informed of his mortality when he was told that he was made from dust and that he would return to dust.

In order to come to a proper conclusion on the question of man's mortality, it is helpful to know the definition of the word "soul," and the Bible provides the answer. In Genesis 2, the Bible says that God formed man from the dust of the ground, but man was not yet alive. Then God breathed into his nostrils the breath of life, and man "became" a living soul. That scripture is as important for what it doesn't say as it is for what it does say. It doesn't say that God inserted a soul into man as a separate entity that could escape from the body and float around in space or in heaven when a person dies. According to the definition in that text, a soul is the union of a body and the breath of life given by God. If you remove either one of those two components, the soul ceases to exist. The only thing that survives when we die is the breath of life that God gave us in the beginning. The Bible says that the living know that they shall die, but the dead know not anything.

When Jesus said that those who were in their graves would hear his voice, he also indicated that there would be two separate resurrections. Those who have done good things will be in the first resurrection, which he calls the resurrection of life. Those who have done evil will be in the second one, which he calls the resurrection of damnation. Paul essentially said the same thing when he said that those who had died in Christ would rise to meet him in the air where they will be joined by the righteous ones who are still alive at the time. There is no mention of sinners being resurrected at that time because they will be raised later to receive their punishment. Revelation 20 also mentions two resurrections, one for the righteous and one for the wicked. As you can see from those Bible texts, we don't go to heaven one person at a time. We all go together as a group.

There are many other Bible passages that make it clear that we do not go to heaven as soon as we die. In John 14, Jesus is preparing the disciples for his departure from the earth. He knew that the news about his departure would sadden his disciples, so he adds the following words of comfort and hope. He says, "I go to prepare a place for you, and if I go and prepare a place for you, I will come again and receive you unto myself, that where I am there you may be also." Pay close attention to the sequence of events in that statement by Jesus:

1. First, Jesus comes back again.

2. Secondly, he receives his followers unto himself.

3. Then, and only then, he takes them to be where he is in heaven.

4. Finally, it is only after that series of events has occurred that his followers are able to occupy the places that he has prepared for them.

We cannot rearrange that sequence of events to fit our own preconceived ideas about when we go to heaven. Jesus could not have made it any clearer that we go to heaven only *after* he returns. As devoted as the disciples were to Jesus and as close as they were to him, even they won't go to heaven until Jesus comes back again, and scriptures are very consistent on this point. Another text that confirms this point is Acts 2:29 and 34 where, hundreds of years after King David's death, Peter says the following: "David ... is both dead and buried, and his sepulchre is with us unto this day.... For David is not ascended into the heavens."

As a further example, Christ was a close friend of Mary, Martha, and their brother, Lazarus. At one point, Lazarus became sick and died. When Lazarus had been dead for four days, Jesus went to Bethany where the grieving sisters lived. When he saw Martha, he didn't try to comfort her by telling her that her brother was alive and well and in heaven already. He certainly would have told her that if it were true. Instead, he told her that her brother would rise again. Martha replied by saying that she knew he would rise again at the resurrection on the "last" day. On another occasion, Jesus was also talking about the resurrection at the end of the world when he said the following about those who believe on him: "I will raise [them] up at the 'last' day" (John 6:40). So both Martha and Jesus had a clear understanding that those who are dead are not in heaven. It is a popular misconception that those who die go immediately to heaven, but this is not true. Instead, they remain in their graves and will not live again in heaven or anywhere else until the resurrection on the "last" day of earth's history.

In addition, the Bible says in Daniel 7:10 that "the judgment was set and the books were opened." That text implies that there would be a particular time when Christ would begin to judge the world. Even though that implication is contrary to popular belief, it is definitely true. For thousands of years, the population of the earth has been so large that many thousands of people die every single day. If people go directly to heaven as soon as they die, that death rate would make it necessary for there to be many thousands of individual judgments made each and every day to determine who will go to heaven and who will not--but that is not what happens. According to the Bible, there is a specific period of time reserved for a single judgment near the end of the world. At some point, the judgment period will end, and Christ will say, "He that is unjust, let him be unjust still; and he that is filthy, let him be filthy still; and he that is righteous, let him be righteous still; and he that is holy, let him be holy still, and behold, I come quickly, and my reward is with me to give every man according as his works shall be" (Revelation 22). So, according to that text, rewards are given out "to every man" when Jesus returns, and not when a person dies.

Further clarification on this point is provided below as I answer some frequently asked questions about what happens to people when they die.

Question:

What about the text where Jesus said to the thief who was about to die along with him on Mt. Calvary: "Truly, I say to you, today you will be with me in Paradise" (Luke 23:43, RSV)? Doesn't that prove that people go to heaven as soon as they die?

Answer:

No, and here is why I say that. The original scriptures were written without punctuation, and the translators put in punctuation where they thought it should be. In this case, the translator made a mistake and put the comma in the wrong place. The comma should go after the word "today" instead of before it. The text has a totally different meaning when the comma is put in the proper place ("Truly, I say to you today, you will be with me in Paradise"). Proof that the dying thief didn't go to heaven on the day he died can be found in the words of Jesus after the resurrection. When Mary saw Jesus early Sunday morning, she was so glad to see him that she wanted to hug him, but he told her not to do so. The reason he gave her was that he had not yet ascended to the Father. If Jesus didn't go to heaven on the day he died, it is certain that the thief didn't go either. When properly understood, the scriptures are very consistent on this point.

Question:

What about Paul's statement where he says that to be absent from the body is to be present with the Lord? Doesn't that prove that we go immediately to heaven when we die?

Answer:

No, it doesn't. Even Christ didn't go to heaven when he died; otherwise, he would not have said what he did to Mary at the tomb. In addition, in 2 Corinthians 12, Paul mentions that he once had a vision in which he was taken to heaven. In describing the experience, he said that he couldn't be certain whether he was in the body or out of the body. It is possible that he was alluding to that kind of experience when he made his statement about being absent from the body and present with the Lord. The more likely possibility is that he was simply stating that if he were to die he would be asleep in Jesus and the very next thing he would be aware of would be the presence of the Lord at the resurrection. Support for this latter possibility is found in another statement by Paul where he says that the "dead in Christ" will rise first during the resurrection, and one of the first things they will see and be aware of is Jesus Christ returning to earth (1 Thessalonians 4:16). In order to conclude that we are immediately "present with the Lord" when we die, one would have to totally ignore the numerous Bible texts that say otherwise.

Finally, the Bible says in Revelation 11 that at a certain point in time (after the events in that prophecy have occurred), the dead will be judged and given their reward. The events in that prophecy have not yet been fulfilled. At the time when that prophecy will be fulfilled, all of the people who died previously are still in their graves. They have not yet been judged, nor have they gone to heaven and received their reward. Even the saints and prophets have not yet been judged and given their rewards. So that Bible text alone dispels the popular belief that we are judged as soon as we die and that we are given our reward immediately.

As you can see, the belief that we go to heaven when we die is a direct contradiction of everything that Jesus, Paul, and the Bible have to say on the subject. There are many false doctrines being taught about those who are dead, and we must be careful not to follow any of those cunningly devised fables. The scriptures alone should be our guide on this and all other doctrines.

God's Commandment Concerning Giving

Another distinguishing feature of the Adventist church is the fact that we follow God's instructions about tithing as found in the third chapter of Malachi. Those instructions are as follows:

> "Bring ye all the tithes into the storehouse that there may be meat in [my] house, and prove me now herewith saith the Lord if I will not open [to] you the windows of heaven and pour you out [such] a blessing that there shall not be room enough to receive it."

For those who are not familiar with tithing, the tithe is ten percent of one's income that is to be given to the church to support its work. Who wouldn't want a superabundance of blessings poured out into their lives, and yet there are those who read those verses and say, "I can't afford to give that much to the church. I need every penny I earn." If I hear people say that, my reply is, "Didn't you just read the ironclad guarantee that comes with paying tithes, and don't you realize who it is that backs up that guarantee?" At that point, it becomes a question of whether you trust yourself and your money more than you trust God and trust his promises. God does not even ask us to trust him in this matter. Instead, he challenges us to try him and see if he won't do what he says. It is so sweet to free yourself from anxieties about money and to rest on God's promises.

I can tell you from personal experience that I have been paying tithes for over 60 years, and I have never missed it. God has never failed to keep his promise in this regard. As my story unfolds, you will see abundant evidence of that. There are only two ways to live our lives: God's way or our way. Make the right choice! You'll be much happier if you do.

All of God's commandments are for our benefit, and only good things can come from our obedience to them. God doesn't ask us to pay our tithe to him because he needs it. He does it to help us place our trust in him instead of in our money. Trust in him grows stronger and stronger as we see him deliver on his promises day after day and year after year. It frees one from stress and anxiety to know that in response to your demonstration of faith in him, God is taking extraordinary measures to ensure that your needs are met. God will enable you to do so much more with 90 percent of your income than you could ever do with your money even if you kept all 100 percent of it.

When you pay tithes, the blessings will come to you regardless of your motives for doing so because God cannot lie, but I urge you not to pay tithes simply for the promised blessings, but because you love God and delight to do all that he asks of you.

The preceding pages provided information about some of the more distinctive doctrines of the Adventist Church. Other than those basic differences, Adventists are much like any other Christian denomination. I hope I've said enough to pique your interest in Adventism, and I invite everyone to visit the nearest Adventist Church and fellowship with us. Visitors are always welcome.

The Adventist Church Becomes My Big and Wonderful Extended Family

When the tent meetings were finally over, regular weekly worship services were moved to Ethnan Temple SDA Church, which was then located at the intersection of Center Avenue and Morgan Street. Interestingly, the church building was located right around the corner from where I used to live eight years earlier as a small child with the Williams family. I was aware of the building when I was a child, but I knew nothing about its occupants and could never have imagined that it would one day be my church.

When I started attending the church each week, I found the members to be so very warm and friendly. It was like I had become part of a large family. Members took a genuine interest in me personally. They invited me into their homes and into their activities both at church and elsewhere. If there was a church-related meeting or event that took place locally or out of town, I was invited to go along and transportation was provided. I loved the music, the preaching, the fellowship, and everything about my local church.

I also enjoyed the annual camp meetings at one of our boarding schools in Pine Forge, Pennsylvania. Those meetings brought thousands of Adventists together from a five- or six-state region for a week of singing, preaching, fellowship, and spiritual renewal. I also enjoyed the worldwide youth congress and the periodic general conference session. These events brought Adventist delegates from all around the world. Those were exciting times for a new believer who was both young in age and in the faith.

The local church held an oratorical contest for which the young people in the church were to be the contestants. The subject of the contest was to be temperance, with the emphasis on the dangers of smoking and drinking. The pastor asked me to participate. I agreed and wrote out my speech. Pastor Cox was absolutely wonderful to me. He treated me the same way any father would treat his own son. About a week or two before the contest, the pastor asked to see a copy of my speech. When he read it, he said that it was very good, but being the gifted orator that he was, he saw ways in which it could be improved. He did a virtual rewrite of the speech and then devoted hours of his time listening to me practice and offering suggestions on how to improve my delivery. Then he did something that absolutely astounded me. He saw that I didn't own a suit, so he took me to a clothing store and bought me a dark suit. When I stepped onto the stage the night of the competition, I was so well coached that I won first prize. The announcement of my victory by the judges was greeted with thunderous applause by the audience. It was a truly exhilarating moment for me.

Church members drove me to the regional competition in Akron, Ohio, where I was to compete against other contestants from a five-state region. Becoming an Adventist opened a whole new world for me. Until that time, I had spent all of my life within the city of Pittsburgh. Now I was traveling to distant cities and states and meeting a lot of different people. God was expanding my horizons at just the time I needed it in order to prepare me for what lay ahead years later.

For some reason, the contest was held in a private home instead of at the church. One contestant after another gave their speeches. When my turn came, I stepped forward and gave it my best, but first prize went to a local girl from Akron. Those in the audience thought I had won, and they were stunned by the decision of the judges. I guess it shouldn't have been too surprising. All of the judges were from Akron, and they were obviously biased toward one of their own. At least that was how I could console myself. The outcome bothered my supporters from Pittsburgh more than it did me. Being new at public speaking and a bit shy about being in front of an audience, I was relieved when it was over. However, the experience did prove to be a major advance in my personal development.

Looking back on this and other experiences, I can see that much of what was happening to me was beyond my control and not of my devising—and that's a good thing. I would never have conceived some of the things that God was to take me through. All I had to do was to follow his lead and give every situation my very best effort. In the book of Proverbs, God has promised that if we will acknowledge him, he will direct our path. Following him has been far more rewarding than anything I could have conceived by myself.

When I announced to my foster mother that I had joined the Adventist Church and could no longer eat pork and certain other foods, she emphatically informed me that she was not going to change the way she cooked her food. I could either eat it or go hungry. I accepted what she said, and for the next few days I didn't eat very much. After several days of this, she realized that I was committed to my faith and was not going to relent. She began to feel sorry for me and gave me money to buy whatever I wanted. I had virtually no experience at cooking food, and menu planning was a big responsibility to have thrust on me so suddenly. For a few days, I ate a lot of peanut butter and honey sandwiches made with whole wheat bread.

When the church heard about my difficulties in practicing my faith in my foster home, Pastor Cox went into action. He inquired among the church members to see if there was a family who would be willing to take me in as a foster child. Mr. and Mrs. Floyd Patterson agreed to do so. He then contacted the orphanage, and they made arrangements for my transfer to an Adventist home in Deanwood, a middle-class suburb outside of Pittsburgh. It made for a long commute to high school in the city every day, but it was such a lovely community that I didn't mind the inconvenience. So now, for the fourth time in my young life, I was in yet another foster home. Psychologists will tell you that children need stability in their lives and that such disruptions can be harmful. It can make the child feel insecure and unloved. It had no such effect on me. I had all of the love and attention I needed in each situation, and I actually thrived in each home. The Pattersons were a joyful elderly couple who were easy to talk to, and they made me feel at home right away.

I spent my senior year in high school living with the Pattersons. When I graduated, I had no idea what I would do. I certainly had no plans to go to college. In those days, I didn't do any long-range planning. I simply took one day at a time. It was time for God to step in and reveal what he had in mind for me next, and so he did. Pastor Cox was impressed with my speaking skills and my spirituality, and he thought I should become a minister. I don't remember if he asked me if I wanted to go to college or not. It was more like he told me I was going, and so I did. He had increasingly become more like a father to me, and I valued his opinion. I later realized that I was not called to be a minister, but I definitely needed to be at the college where he would send me. He sent me to Oakwood College, our denomination's college in Huntsville, Alabama.

Pastor Cox's influence on my life and my future was invaluable to me. Without his involvement in my life at that particular time, I would not be the person I am today. So many wonderful things that happened to me are a direct result of his decision to send me to Oakwood. I didn't know it at the time, but he was a visible manifestation of God's unseen hand in my life.

Church members provided me with a steamer trunk, helped me pack, and purchased a bus ticket for me. They also gave me a small sum of money to take with me. The amount of money was not nearly enough to pay for my tuition, but there would be work available for me on campus. I later learned that many students were able to earn all or a major part of their tuition by finding jobs on or off campus.

At age 18, I was officially out from under the care of the orphanages and was completely on my own for the first time in my life.

I never once worried about how I would survive. Christ said that we are not to take anxious thought about where we will live or what we will eat or wear for clothing. God knows we have need of those things and will provide what we need—and so he did, as I will reveal later. All I had to do was look for opportunities, and sometimes I didn't even have to look for them. They often presented themselves to me.

Mrs. Patterson had been very good to me, and our parting was a mixture of joy and sadness for both of us. There was a crowd of church members that gathered at the Pattersons' home to see me off. Someone in the crowd asked me if there was anything that I would like to take with me. I said, "Yes." Pointing to Mrs. Patterson, I said, "Her." Everyone had a good laugh. Mrs. Patterson was totally surprised and delighted; she laughed, too, but I think I also saw a tear in her eye.

Chapter Two

I Love Pittsburgh, PA

Why do I love the city of Pittsburgh so much? They took complete responsibility for my care from age two to eighteen, and they did an outstanding job by working hard to make sure I had every possible chance to succeed in life. I realize that the funding probably came from Allegheny County, so I want to give them credit for their part in it, but it was the hardworking and dedicated professionals in Pittsburgh who administered the program. So detailed and thorough was their program that I got the best possible preparation for adulthood.

The city carefully screened and selected potential foster parents and then paid them a certain amount of money to care for each child. Not only that, but they had a clothing center in the orphanage building to which our foster parents could bring us twice a year for brand new summer and winter clothing. The orphanage also had a dentist and a doctor on the staff, and we could go to them for annual checkups or as necessary for acute medical problems.

In addition to all of that, they arranged for us to go to camp for two weeks every summer. Those camp experiences were unforgettably wonderful. There was hiking, swimming, boating, archery, bonfires, singing, and great food. There was a girls' camp on the other side of the lake, and on the last weekend of the camp, they brought us together for a party and a dance. I have a painful memory from one of those dances. We were all seated in a big circle around the dance floor. I had never danced before, so I just sat and watched everyone else having fun on the dance floor. A rather cute girl came over and asked me to dance with her. When I explained to her that I didn't know how to dance, she offered to teach me. After I stepped on her feet numerous times, she gave up the effort. That was a painful moment for both of us—physically for her and emotionally for me. In all of the years since that event, I have never once stepped onto a dance floor.

One of my favorite songs that I learned at camp was called *Evening Prayer*, and all these years later, I still occasionally sing it to myself. Both the words and the music are beautiful and profoundly moving. The words to it are as follows:

Evening Prayer

If I have wounded any soul today,
If I have caused one foot to go astray,
If I have walked in my own willful way,
Dear Lord, forgive!

If I have uttered idle words or vain,
If I have turned aside from want or pain,
Lest I myself shall suffer through the strain,
Dear Lord, forgive!

We would sing that song every night, either outdoors around a bonfire or in the dining hall. It was a wonderful way to end each day.

In my opinion, the school system in Pittsburgh is one of the best in the world. Other cities would do well to imitate their model. No other system could possibly have given me a better preparation for life. In addition to teaching us the usual academic courses such as English, math, science, geography, history, music, and so forth, they taught us some very practical things that we would need for everyday life and for good health. Physical education was much more than just fun and games in the gym. We had classroom studies where we learned the health benefits of regular exercise. We also learned the specific nutrients required by the body to maintain good health, and we learned the foods that would best supply those nutrients. We also learned what foods and harmful practices to avoid.

In home economics class, both boys and girls learned how to cook meals and how to clean and manage a home. In business class, we learned many things that businesspersons need to know. In economics class, we learned how to prepare a budget and how to manage money wisely. We also learned typing skills, which helped prepare us to type our term papers and helped many people find jobs.

One of the most important things that the Pittsburgh public school system did was to require that all boys, whether they were going to college or not, had to take three vocational shops: woodworking, metal working, and printing. We also learned the basics of electrical wiring and plumbing. Those shops greatly enhanced the opportunities for boys to find employment if there were no jobs in the field for which college prepared them. They provided an excellent backup plan and gave boys the reassurance that they would always be able to provide for themselves and their families.

The skills I learned in woodworking shop were invaluable. They could have prepared me to pursue further training and a career in that field. Even though I didn't do that, I did spend many enjoyable hours with it as a hobby. I put a workshop in my basement and made many fine pieces of furniture and other items. I was very comfortable making repairs around the house and putting a new roof on our porch. I worked with a confidence that I would not have had if it had not been for the class in woodworking. I was even able to earn a part-time living by doing remodeling work while I was in college. In metal shop, I learned how to cut, bend, and shape metal for many different projects. I am eternally grateful to God for giving me those skills so early in life. Only he could know how much I would need and enjoy those skills in the future.

The one shop that I absolutely fell in love with was the print shop. I loved every aspect of the printing press and bindery work such as paper cutting, binding books and magazines, and punching or drilling holes where needed. I also enjoyed the various methods of typesetting (we didn't have computers back in those days). Once the teacher had taught us the basic skills, he allowed us to create any kind of printed product we desired. One of the things I produced was a pamphlet about the history of our high school based on my research. It even had illustrations throughout. My teacher was so impressed that he suggested that I should take a copy of it to the librarian. I did, and she made it available to all who wanted to read it. Among the other items I produced was a multi-colored greeting card. The print shop really stimulated my imagination and stirred up my creative side. I enjoyed printing so much that I chose it as an elective course every semester all through my years in high school.

My print shop teacher in high school was Royal J. Hartwick, and he had a small print shop in the basement of his home. He was so impressed with my skills and enthusiasm that he invited me to work in his home print shop during the summer following my junior year. It was fun taking the long trolley ride to his home in the suburbs every day. He would meet me when I got off the trolley and take me to his house. His wife always greeted me warmly, and I felt very comfortable being there. A teenager could not have asked for a better summer job. The amazing thing is that I didn't seek that job. It sought me. There is no doubt in my mind that God's hand was involved in it.

The following summer, Mr. Hartwick's shop didn't have enough business for him to hire me again, but he recommended me to two friends of his who also had a print shop in another part of town, and they hired me during my last summer before I went off to college.

School systems that focus solely on academics do their students and society a distinct disservice. While we do have to compete with the rest of the world on academic subjects, we also need the more practical subjects that will really be useful to us in everyday life. Those courses were a part of the curriculum in the Pittsburgh school system when I was a student there in the 1940s and 1950s. I hope that nothing has changed that outstanding school system.

Pittsburgh provides a very comprehensive education for its young people and gives wonderful care to its orphans, but I love the city for more than just those government services alone. I love it because of the citizens of Pittsburgh who opened their homes and their hearts to me at the most vulnerable point in my life. I also love it for the way in which the community of churches embraced me and gave me a moral code by which to conduct my life. They also gave meaning, purpose, and direction to my life. Those are the reasons why I am proud to say that I love the city of Pittsburgh.

Chapter Three

College, Career, and Family

College Days

God used college to bring me to a whole new level of maturity and to prepare me for my life's work. Although college would provide me with a good education, that is not what helped me find my career. As you will see from this section of the book, God used a rather unusual method to launch my career, but I had to be at Oakwood College at this specific time in order for it to happen, and that is something that only God could have arranged.

In late August of 1955, church members drove me to the Greyhound bus station in Pittsburgh and gave me a loving sendoff. After the goodbyes and well wishes were said, I boarded the bus with all of my worldly possessions, and soon I was on my way to begin a totally new phase of my life.

I had never been on an interstate highway bus of this type before, so it was a totally new experience for me. The trip was pleasant enough as we rolled through one state after another. That is until we reached Nashville, Tennessee. The Greyhound bus line only went that far, and I had to transfer to the Trailways bus line, which covered the southern states. In my naiveté, I took the third seat from the front of the bus. When the bus driver saw where I was sitting, he came over to me and in a disdainful way said, "How about you going to the back of the bus with the rest of the colored folks!" Fortunately for me, I was young and compliant when told to do something by an adult. If it had been at a later point in my life, I might have refused to move. God had a destiny and a timetable for me, and it was not for me to be in a prison or grave in Tennessee. It would be left for Rosa Parks to take that kind of stand just a few years later.

This was my first exposure to racism. Having grown up in the north, I never knew there was such a thing as racial segregation. The rest of the trip was uneventful, and before long, I found myself on the campus of Oakwood College in Huntsville, Alabama.

Located in a semi-rural area, the campus was absolutely beautiful. The major buildings had colonial style columns and were arranged in a huge oval. They were nestled among numerous stately oak trees from which the college got its name.

There is an interesting historical note about how the college was founded. In the late nineteenth century, racial segregation was rife in America, and it was difficult for people of color to obtain an education. At that time, the Adventist denomination had a prophetess named Ellen G. White. She had a vision in which she was shown that a school needed to be established to provide educational opportunities for African-American Adventists. She was also shown the exact spot where the school should be located in northern Alabama. In her vision, she saw angels walking among the oak trees on the site. The spot indeed does appear to have been divinely inspired. The college was founded in 1896, and it continues to flourish all these years later as it faithfully carries out its mission.

I was fortunate to arrive just as the building contractor was putting the finishing touches on a brand new dormitory for men. I was one of the first occupants of Peterson Hall, which was named after a very distinguished former president of the college. I got settled into my dorm room and started to get acclimated to life in college. Since Oakwood is a religious institution, students are required to assemble twice a day in their respective dormitories for morning and evening worship. Also, a certain number of religion courses were required as a part of the curriculum. This was the perfect environment for a young, newly-baptized Adventist, and I thrived in it. Pastor Cox knew what was best for me when he sent me there. Those things didn't just happen to me by coincidence. I am fully convinced that they were guided by God's unseen hand.

When I first moved into the dormitory, I discovered that Maurice Murphy had been assigned to be my roommate. Maurice quickly determined that I was too square, too nerdy, and too uncool to be his roommate. He requested to be reassigned to another room so he could be with Bert Reid who was someone he had known before. At first, I was a little bit bothered by the fact that he had moved out so quickly without really getting to know me, but God's hand was even in that incident, and he knew what was best for me.

The next person who was assigned to my room was Robert Taylor. Robert was a self-confident, outgoing, six-foot tall fellow. He was a theology major who was studying to be a minister, and he was also a talented musician. He played the piano a little bit. He also had a deep bass voice, and soon he was singing with one of the many male quartets on campus. We both felt perfectly comfortable sharing living quarters.

Robert came from a solid middle-class background and was very far ahead of me culturally. He was shocked to find out that I didn't know what classical music was and that I had never heard of Beethoven, Bach, Schubert, Mozart, or any of the other great classical musicians. He taught me that there were certain basic pieces of classical music that everyone should know about—pieces such as Beethoven's *Fifth Symphony, Moonlight Sonata,* and many others. He also introduced me to some more modern classics such as Gershwin's *Rhapsody in Blue,* which I had never heard before. Robert loaned me his many LP albums so I could listen to them and become acquainted with the music of the great masters. Because of Robert, I have had a lifelong and deep appreciation of classical music, and my life has been greatly enriched thereby. God knew what I needed at that stage of my development, and he wove it into my life seamlessly.

The nearly 1,200 students at Oakwood came from all over the United States and many came from foreign countries. The college was small enough that we all got to know each other on sight and often by name. Everyone was so friendly that it felt like we were one big family. In fact, if we got to know someone especially well, we became unofficial relatives (campus mothers, fathers, sons, daughters, cousins, uncles, aunts, etc.). Some 58 years later, I still keep in touch with my campus "mom," so great was the bond of the friendships we formed in college.

A couple of highly revered elderly ladies lived on the campus in retirement, and their lives were an inspiration to all of us. The first one was Eugenia Cunningham, whom everyone affectionately called "Mother Cunningham." She had a son who was a prominent minister of whom she was very proud. Judging from her age, she would have been around before Oakwood was founded in the late 1800s. The other distinguished lady was Anna Knight, who had spent many years overseas as a missionary. The lives of those women were an inspiration for the students to live out the school's motto, "Enter to learn, and go forth to serve."

There were numerous employment opportunities on or near the campus that gave the students a chance to earn enough money to pay for all or part of their education. As a result, most of them were able to leave college without any lingering debt. The school had a huge agricultural and dairy farm that provided job opportunities for students. Although a large percentage of the produce and dairy products were consumed in the school's cafeteria, I believe that a substantial portion of it may have been sold commercially to provide revenue for the school. The school also had a commercial laundry and dry cleaning plant that employed many students and brought in tremendous profits for the school. One of its most lucrative contracts was one to do all of the laundry and dry cleaning for military personnel stationed at Redstone Arsenal. Students found employment in the campus store, the bakery, the cafeteria, the library, the custodial department, the various offices, and in lawn care services. There were many other work opportunities too numerous to mention. There was so much industry going on that one could almost feel sorry for the poor little rich kids who didn't have to work.

By God's providence, the school had a fully-equipped print shop, but nobody on campus knew anything about printing or how to operate the equipment. Professor Charles E. Galley was in charge of the print shop and probably knew how to operate it, but his teaching duties in the business education department kept him too busy to spend any time in the shop. So the print shop sat idle just waiting for my arrival. Some would call it luck, but I know better. My retrospective look at life allows me to see a consistent pattern that can't be explained away by mere luck. Mr. Galley was ecstatic when he learned that I had experience as a printer. To this day, I'm not really sure how he found out about my skills. After all, I was one of several hundred new students arriving on campus. Perhaps he saw my high school transcript. He immediately put me in charge of the print shop. I was thrilled to find that my love for printing could find expression there in college. I was back in my element once again.

For a long time, I was the only employee in the shop. About a year later, another experienced student arrived from Africa, and the two of us worked together.

The new arrival was Hume Siwundhla. Hume was a mild-mannered and soft-spoken man. There was a bit of shyness in his personality as well. By contrast, he was married to a vivacious and outgoing lady named Princess Alice. Everybody called her Princess Alice, but the word "Princess" was not her first name—it was her title. As a daughter of African royalty, she was a true princess. The Siwundhlas were just two of many foreign students who added a rich diversity to the school. During my time at Oakwood, a number of nationally famous pop singers and one rock-and-roll singer converted to Adventism and came to Oakwood as students. Among them were Joyce Bryant, Shirley Verette, and Little Richard. They had given up their worldly careers to follow Christ. It was quite exciting to see these celebrities around the campus, to hear their testimonies about how they came to know the Lord, and to hear them sing gospel songs instead of the rock-and-roll and pop songs that had made them famous. I especially enjoyed hearing Joyce sing the song entitled "I'd Rather Have Jesus." That song became the theme of her new life in Christ. It also explained why she was willing to give up the money, glitz, and glamour of show business in order to serve Christ and gain treasures in heaven.

There were many concerts, banquets, parties, guest lectures, sporting events, roller skating nights, and other events that provided plenty of opportunities for dating. There were also numerous attractive, intelligent, and godly women from which to choose. I didn't do any dating in high school, but I took to it with alacrity in college. I even fell in and out of love a couple of times. I was nowhere near being ready for matrimony. Although none of the relationships led to marriage, I did make many friendships that have lasted throughout my life, and I still keep in touch with a number of friends from college. Oakwood was the absolute best environment for me to be in at that stage of my life. I was among so many people who shared my values and my faith. I could not have known about the place or chosen it on my own, but God knew about it. It was no accident that I was there. I was right where God wanted me to be, and he got me there without any effort on my part. This is one of the many instances when God brought someone into my life and used them to steer me in the right direction. I shudder to think of what I might have missed out on if I had followed my own path instead of listening to Pastor Cox.

I settled into the routine of going to classes, and things were going rather well for me. I started out as a theology major, and I was getting mostly "A" grades in my classes, including my Greek language class. I spent most of my spare time working in the print shop.

After several months, my funds began to run low in spite of my work at the print shop. There was a real possibility that I might have to drop out of school. However, my church family back in Pittsburgh had not forgotten about me. When they heard about my situation, those wonderful people organized a fundraiser at church and called it "Oscar Daniels Day." I was amazed to be the recipient of such great love. After all, I had only been in their midst for two years.

I made it through the first year of college, and as the summer break approached, I had to decide what I would do during that time. Right on cue, an opportunity presented itself. The Adventist church publishes many books and magazines, and they employ leaders to recruit sales people to sell those materials. Those sales people are known as "literature evangelists." One such leader was George Anderson from Ohio. Toward the end of the school year, he came down to the college to pick up his daughter, Beverly. While he was there, he came to one of the assemblies attended by the entire student body. He asked if anyone wanted to sell books in Ohio during the summer. I had never been a salesman before, and I have no idea why I agreed to go with him, but I did. Perhaps he offered to train us.

When the school year ended in May of 1956, I got ready for the long ride to Columbus, Ohio, where I would plunge into a line of work that was totally new to me—that of being a door-to-door salesman. Mr. Anderson loaded me and Beverly into the car for the trip. Along with us were the two or three other students that Mr. Anderson had recruited.

Mr. Anderson had made arrangements for me to have a room in the home of Mr. and Mrs. Neil, who were members of the Adventist Church in Columbus. The Neils gave me a warm reception and made me feel welcome in their home and in their lives. Their three sons also made me feel welcome, and I enjoyed getting to know them. Daniel was the oldest, and his career path led him to follow his father into working at an automobile plant or some similar factory there in Columbus. Richard was the second oldest son. He was studying to be a doctor, and years later, he established a very successful practice in California. The youngest son was Fred. I don't know what line of work he went into, but four years later, in 1960, we both got drafted into the army and ended up receiving basic training at the same army base. We were sent to different locations after basic training, and I lost track of him after that.

Guided by An Unseen Hand

Mr. Anderson's method of teaching me to be a salesman was very novel and very effective. I went with him from door to door in my assigned territory. For the first three days, he did all of the talking and asked me to just observe his technique. When someone opened the door to us, he briefly explained why we were there and asked if we might come in to make our presentation. He gave a very effective pitch explaining how beneficial it would be to have the books in their home. The man was an absolute master of handling reluctance and of closing the sale. At the end of each presentation, he offered them a free Bible study course that they could complete at home in their spare time by simply mailing in the completed lessons in order to receive the next lesson. I thoroughly absorbed his whole approach to selling.

After I had observed him for three days, Mr. Anderson asked me if I wanted to do the next presentation while he observed me. With only a little bit of trepidation, I mimicked what I had seen him do successfully so many times, and I got a sale on my first attempt. After that, I was off and running. I became one of the leading sales people among the students who worked for Mr. Anderson that summer.

I was astounded that a good 70 to 80 percent of the people who heard my presentation ended up buying one or more of my books. Among the books I sold was a "Tiny Tots" set of Bible story books for very small children and another set for older children. I was even able to sell a set of the Tiny Tot books to a pregnant woman whose first child had not even been born yet. I convinced her that she needed to have it available just as soon as the child was ready for it. It would be easy to attribute such success to my own skills and efforts, but a retrospective look at my life shows clearly that God gives me whatever skills I need for every new situation in which I find myself. All I have to do is step out in faith and seize the opportunity that he presents to me.

An interesting situation occurred when I entered a young lady's apartment to sell my books. Her boyfriend happened to be there when I made my presentation. He tried to dissuade her from buying my books, but she was convinced of their worth and she bought them over his objections. He continued to mutter and fume about the matter, but his girlfriend had a mind of her own and acted on her convictions. Needless to say, I was greatly relieved to exit that apartment.

Walton Whaley was my roommate at the Neils' home. He was a fellow student from Oakwood who was also a book salesman working for Mr. Anderson that summer. The two of us made so much money that summer that we used some of it to go half and half on the purchase of a used car. Daniel Neil was kind enough and patient enough to teach me how to drive and help me get my driver's license. One day when I wanted to practice my driving skills, a friend took me to a popular park in Columbus. As I was driving along the winding road in the park, I went just a hair over the center line as I was passing a car traveling in the opposite direction. When I did that, I scraped the other car ever so slightly. Of all the cars in Columbus, I just happened to hit this particular one. It was driven by the boyfriend of the girl who had bought my book over his objections. When he got out of the car and recognized me, all he could say was, "You!!" After I apologized and he got over the shock of seeing me again, we assessed the situation. There was no actual damage to either car, and there was only a one-foot long paint mark on his car. He estimated that it could be touched up for ten to twenty dollars. I paid him on the spot and he never pursued the matter any further. After I sold the book to his girlfriend, I had never expected to see him again, and so it was especially embarrassing to see him under those circumstances.

As pleased as I was with my success as a salesman, the thing that pleases me the most about that summer is the huge number of people that I enrolled in the home study Bible course (my guess is that there were at least 200). Years later, one of our leading evangelists, Charles D. Brooks, conducted a series of evangelistic meetings in Columbus and baptized more than 200 people. I am certain that many of them were people I had enrolled in the Bible course. The evangelist and his staff would certainly have used their names as leads to follow up on. If so, I may see some people in heaven who will recognize me from that wonderful summer in Columbus.

After I got back to Oakwood in the fall, I completed the first semester's course work. About halfway through the second semester, it became clear that I did not have enough funds to stay in school. I did not notify the Pittsburgh church about my situation. They had already done so much for me. When I dropped out, it meant that I could no longer stay in the dormitory or eat in the cafeteria. Even though I was facing a new dilemma, I never panicked or experienced any anxiety. In ever-changing circumstances, the Lord had a way of providing for my needs so promptly that I never had a need to worry about anything.

In hindsight, I now realize something that I had not noticed before. It is often at times when life seems to be unraveling that God is preparing us for a major change in our lives. If I had been able to stay in school, I would probably have missed what God had in store for me (you will see the evidence of that as my story unfolds). When I look back at my entire life, I am better able to see the consistent pattern of God's involvement in my life, especially at those critical moments. The message that comes through to me is as follows: Don't despair during difficult days. God has not abandoned you and will bring you through those times and will often leave you better off than before. Find rest and peace in that reassurance.

At about that time, I heard of a poor widow who lived about a quarter of a mile from the campus with her three teenaged children. Even though she worked in the college cafeteria, she was struggling to make ends meet. She desperately needed to supplement her income. She let it be known that she had rooms for rent in her home for $10 a month (that doesn't seem like much, but in 1957, it went a long way). Her name was Hortense Davis, and she lived in a row of connected houses that were made of corrugated metal. The community was jokingly called "Tin City." I believe they were hastily constructed after World War II to house some of the many soldiers returning from the war. They ended up becoming permanent housing for some poor families after they were no longer needed by the war veterans. I rented one of the rooms in Mrs. Davis' home. It turned out that it was not a real room in the true sense of the word. Mrs. Davis had partitioned off one end of a large living room with a curtain. Behind the curtain, she had placed two beds, both of which were for rent. It was rather meager, but believe me, I was very happy to have it in view of my dire circumstances.

Mrs. Davis had a greatly disfigured face. I'm not sure whether it was the result of an injury or a stroke. It pulled her mouth to one side, making it difficult for her to open her mouth fully when she smiled, spoke, or laughed. She could only open one side of her mouth, but when she smiled or laughed, the joy and love that she exuded were so infectious and captivating that I usually never even noticed her disfigurements at all. Her three children all attended the junior or senior high school that was a part of the college complex. The children's names were Artie Joel, Charissa, and Pinky Bonita. They were well behaved and a joy to be with. It wasn't long before Mrs. Davis drew me into all of the family activities, and soon I was eating meals with them. I don't know how she made any profit on the little bit of money I paid her each month. I'm sure she operated at a loss.

Mrs. Davis treated me more like a son than a roomer. On one occasion, I mentioned that I needed a lightweight jacket. Before I knew it, she took me to Dunnavant's, a major department store in town, and let me pick out the jacket I wanted. I don't know how she managed it on her income, but she insisted on doing it. Unselfish giving was an integral part of her nature. Another time, I was lamenting the fact that I wanted to take a date to one of the major social events on the campus, but I didn't have the money to do so. Before I knew what was happening, she had gone to a neighbor and borrowed the money for me. It is rare to see such pure and unselfish love. As amazing as those acts of kindness were, she went even further. She told me that if I could find one or two more students to stay with her for $10 a month, I could stay for free. I took advantage of that offer and brought her my good friend Robert Sparks. I now had free room and board with little or no effort on my part. God is truly amazing in the way he provides. There is no way I could have found such a situation on my own. It is abundantly clear to me that I was led there by God's unseen hand.

Another way in which God continued to provide for me was by bringing a job opportunity to my attention before I had even begun looking for work. Mr. Albert Johnson was a kind of handyman and jack of all trades who lived near the edge of the campus. He had negotiated contracts with housing developers to go into the new homes after construction was completed and clean them up to make them ready for occupancy. In order to speed construction of the nearly 200 houses in the development, the developer didn't want to lose time by masking (or covering) all of the windows, bathtubs, bathroom mirrors, etc., before spray painting the rooms, so the painters sprayed the windows as well as the walls in every room of every house. Our job was to come in with single-edged razor blades and scrape the paint off of the windows, mirrors, bathtubs, sinks, and other places where it was not supposed to be. The paint created a seal that caused the windows to be stuck shut. With our razor blades, we had to cut the seal so the windows could be opened. After we removed all of the excess paint, we had to sweep up all of the construction debris, scrub the floors and leave everything clean and spotless. Each of us got $20 per house, and we could complete three to five houses a day during the summer. That earned us sixty to one hundred dollars a day, which was quite a bit of money in those days. Some would even consider it to be good money in today's job market. Such were the blessings that God continually showered on me, and the best was yet to come.

I learned many new and wonderful things when I joined the Adventist Church. As I said before, one thing I learned was the Bible-based principle of tithing (giving a tenth of one's income to God). In Malachi 3:10, God says that if we will faithfully give him ten percent of our income, then he will open the windows of heaven and pour out such copious blessings that we will not be able to receive them all. He even challenges us to try him to see if he will keep that promise. That's a pretty powerful promise that is easy to prove or disprove simply by taking up God's challenge. When I began paying a tenth of my income to the church, I didn't do it because of the benefits that God had promised. I did it because I was committed to doing God's will completely. After faithfully paying my tithe to God for over 60 years, I can say from experience that God most definitely keeps his promise. Take the challenge and see what he'll do for you! Anything that God asks us to do is for our benefit, not his. By paying tithe, we demonstrate that we put our trust in God and not in our money. It also helps us to overcome selfishness and brings us into partnership with God. In addition, it's thrilling to see the myriad ways in which he chooses to bless you. I assure you that you will be amazed.

I was surviving nicely at that time. I had a comfortable place to stay, I received both maternal and familial love in the Davis home, and I had a decent income, but my life basically came to a standstill. I had no significant goals to drive me forward, but God was about to make the major move that would substantially change my life. I'm enjoying this retrospective look at my life because it gives me the big picture and allows me to see things I didn't notice before. As I describe what happened next, see if you can detect God's hand in arranging the things that happened to me. His involvement is oh so obvious to me, and I'm sure you'll see it, too.

Since I was no longer a student, I almost never went into the campus library, but for some unknown reason, I decided to go there on one particular day. Another thing I rarely did was to read the announcements on the bulletin board, but again, for some unknown reason, I did so on that particular day. I was surprised to see on that big four-by-six foot bulletin board that there was only one tiny little announcement that couldn't have been more than two inches wide by two inches in size in very small print. It was a tiny little classified ad that had been clipped from the newspaper. It was so tiny that I might easily have ignored it, but for some unknown reason, I read it.

That ad had no relevance to any other student on campus except me. I believe that I am the only one who noticed it, and I am certainly the only one who acted upon it. The ad announced that the Government Printing Office in Washington, DC, had openings for people interested in a career in the printing business. Only later did I learn that they were going to hire between 100 and 200 people whom they would put through a five-year apprentice program. Upon graduation, they would be given positions as journeymen printers. It was an ongoing program that they repeated every three years or so to have trained people available to replace the older workers who were retiring.

I didn't hesitate. I responded to the ad immediately and notified the printing office of my interest in the position, but I heard nothing from them for a long time. Someone once said that God's purposes know neither haste nor delay, but they always occur on time. That is certainly true. In all of nature, nothing is rushed, and we should learn to live in harmony with the rhythms of nature instead of our own anxieties and fears or the dictates of other things such as our own preferred timetable. The sun rises and sets when it is supposed to. Seasons come and go right on schedule. Crops grow from seeds to roots, sprouts, shoots, and full-grown plants on their own timetable, and nothing can be safely done to speed up that timetable. The offspring of all animals must go through the prescribed gestation period for optimal development. So it is with our lives. God brings things to pass at exactly the right time for our best good. Finally, in God's time, I was notified that I should go to the local post office in Huntsville where I was to take a lengthy written examination. After I did that, it must have been four or five months before I heard anything from them.

I had pretty much forgotten about my application when I received notification that I had been accepted and should report for duty on May 12, 1958. That was the start of what would be an enjoyable and rewarding 28-year career. I have a series of questions that I asked myself, and I pose them to you. What would have happened if I had not received a foundation in printing way back in junior and senior high school? What would have happened if I had not become an Adventist and been sent off to Oakwood College by Pastor Cox? What was it that caused the librarian to be reading the classified ads in the first place? She loved her job and was secure in her position, so I'm sure she wasn't looking for a job for herself. What caused her to cut out that one particular ad and post it on the bulletin board? Why would I go to the library when I had no particular reason to do so? What would cause me to read a bulletin board that I rarely ever read? Normally, the bulletin board was cluttered with dozens of announcements. This ad was made conspicuous by being the only one there that day. If it had been mixed in with dozens of other announcements, would I have taken the time to read all of them and find this one? I know the answers to all of those questions. Now what do you think? Was it just a bunch of lucky coincidences or were things controlled and orchestrated by God in order to get my attention? It would take more faith to believe in luck and coincidence than to believe that God had a hand in it. That was a divine setup if ever I saw one.

I began to wrap up my affairs in Huntsville and to pack my bags for the trip to Washington, DC. The news of my acceptance was wonderful, but the news got even better. When I told Mr. Galley that I was going to be working at the Government Printing Office, he got excited and his eyes lit up. He told me that his mother lived across the street a block away from the office and that he would arrange for me to have a room in her home. On top of that, he offered to drive me to Washington where he would introduce me to his mother and help me get settled in her home.

God says that if we are faithful in paying our tithes that he will open the windows of heaven and pour out such an abundance of blessings that we will not be able to receive them all. In this case, the blessings were so numerous and coming so fast that it was indeed hard to keep up with them all.

The Start of My Career with the Job of My Dreams

Early in the month of May, I said a sad farewell to Mrs. Davis, who had been like a mother to me. Then I was off to work at the world's biggest print shop (at one time it had 8,000 employees). God knew I was not cut out to be a minister. Now I would fulfill my true destiny—the one for which he had been preparing me ever since my first exposure to printing way back in junior high school. It was there that my passion for printing was first ignited.

Mr. Galley's mother was named Luberta George. She was an older and toothless lady who had a jolly soul. She would often say things that would trigger one round of laughter after another. She was an absolute delight to be around, and she immediately made me feel welcome. I was amazed at how the Lord went before me everywhere and prepared the way for me, causing so many people to open their homes to me, even though I was a total stranger to them when I first moved in. Mrs. George lived alone, so she was happy to have someone else in the house, especially a fellow believer who shared her values and with whom she had so much in common.

In spite of her age, Mrs. George owned a car and was still a competent driver. Each Sabbath she took me to the Adventist Church, which was located quite far from where we lived. This home had everything I needed. I had transportation to church, the store, and other places around town. For only $25 a month, I had a comfortable place to live that was only a five-minute walk from my job. I was also within walking distance of many famous places around Washington, including the Capitol, the White House, the Washington Monument, the Lincoln Memorial, and the downtown shopping area. Did all of this just happen by chance, or was it prearranged by God? By now, you know what I think. Now what do you think? I know I use the word "amazing" quite a lot, but it is the word that best describes how wonderfully the Lord provides for my every need.

As you read through the various events in my life, keep asking yourself if they happened by chance or if the hand of God was involved, and see what conclusions you reach. Then see if you have had similar events in your life that you have taken for granted. After looking at the entire span of my life and seeing how God has provided for my every need, I have learned to rely on him completely. That's the lesson that Jesus was trying to teach to his disciples. On one occasion, he was about to send them into distant cities to preach the gospel. Before he sent them on their way, he told them something that defied logic—something that must have puzzled the disciples. He told them not to take any money, food, extra clothing, sermon notes, or weapons with them. He knew that God would supply their every need, but he wanted them to experience it for themselves. When they returned from their travels, he asked them if they lacked anything while they were away, and they said that they lacked nothing. They had learned that they could be free from anxiety about mundane things and could rely on God. It's a lesson we all need to learn. Christ said that not even a sparrow could fall to the earth without God noticing it. Just as surely as God's eye is on the sparrow, his eye is also on you. Just as surely as he provides for the sparrow's needs, he will provide for yours. Even though God provides for the sparrow, he doesn't drop his provisions in the sparrow's nest. The sparrow has to do its part and go out and find it, and so must we. Go forth wherever life may lead you with full confidence that God will provide.

That lesson about reliance on God was a one-time lesson that did not need to be repeated for them or for us. The point had been made for them, and it has been made for us. The next time Jesus sent the disciples out, he told them to take everything they would need, but they would always know that God would supply anything they might need. It is in God that we should place our trust, and not in our own resources.

When I got settled in my new location in Washington, DC, I was pleased to discover that there were 32 Adventist churches in the city and its surrounding suburbs in Maryland and Virginia. Those congregations had very dynamic leadership at all levels, and they were constantly providing different activities for the members to enjoy. There were numerous concerts by talented musicians; inspiring sermons by distinguished guest speakers; annual church picnics; sports teams; sight-seeing trips; hikes through the scenic countryside, woodlands, and mountain areas; annual camp meetings where we would stay in cabins, tents, or dormitories for ten days worshipping and fellowshipping with thousands of other

Adventists from a five- or six-state region; and regular weekly church services. This is just a partial list of the many activities sponsored by the various churches.

Another church-sponsored activity that I thoroughly enjoyed was the occasional bike rides. There are numerous bike trails going north into Maryland and south into Virginia (some go to historic places such as George Washington's home in Mt. Vernon, Virginia). My favorite bike trail was the one that ran parallel to the C&O Canal in Maryland. There was a bike rental shop at one point along the canal. Scores of us would rent bikes there and spend the entire day riding through the scenic woodlands that extended for many miles on both sides of the canal.

Years later when I got married, and had children, we bought our own bikes and traveled various bike trails as a family. I also had a co-worker who was an avid bike rider. He and I would go on 25- or 30-mile bike trips along Maryland's eastern shore. Those were glorious times riding along hour after hour with the Atlantic Ocean on one side and beautiful rural scenery on the other. The Lord continually brought to my attention activities and people he knew I would enjoy, and he made them available to me. At the time, I took it all for granted. Looking back on it in hindsight, I now realize that God was abundantly fulfilling his promise to pour out his blessings on those who are faithful. I no longer take those things for granted. Instead I live in grateful amazement at all that he has done and continues to do on a daily basis. Now I know why King David wrote over 70 psalms giving praise and thanks to God. He had an acute awareness of God's involvement in his life. He saw God's goodness in the sky above, in all of nature, and in all of God's provisions for his needs. How wonderful it would be if our eyes could be opened and we could see the goodness of the Lord as clearly as David did.

Things were going very well at my new job. There are many branches of the Government Printing Office scattered across the country, but the central office consists of three massive red-brick buildings that rise eight stories high. They occupy one whole city block plus parking lots that occupy another two or three city blocks. I walked into one of those massive buildings on Monday, May 12, 1958, and began what would be 28 of the most exciting and enjoyable years of my life. The program required that I and the others in my group go through a five-year apprenticeship. During those five years, we were to receive training or observe the work being done in all production areas of the building including typesetting, proofreading, camera room, the bindery, the press room, and the plate-making room (those metal plates are the image-transfer sheets that go on the printing presses and transfer the printed images onto paper). After observing us as apprentices for two years, the office would place us in the department for which we showed the greatest aptitude or where we were needed the most. There we would receive three years of intensive specialized training. After that time, we would be placed in permanent jobs as journeyman printers. I really wanted to operate the big printing presses, but my aptitude results showed that I was best suited to be a typesetter. That turned out to be a very good choice for me, and I excelled at it. Proofreaders told me that they liked to read my work because it was usually free of any typographical errors when compared to the work produced by other typesetters. Those typing classes I took way back in high school gave me a real advantage in this job. Was I just lucky that way, or did the Lord foresee what lay ahead and give me the best possible preparation for it? You already know what I think, so I'll just leave it to you to draw your own conclusions.

When I got established in my new job and started receiving regular paychecks, I periodically sent money to Mrs. Davis. No matter how much I sent, however, I could never repay the love and kindness she showed to me. When I showed up at her doorstep, I was a virtual stranger to her. She may have seen me when she was serving food in the school cafeteria, but she didn't really know me. That didn't matter to her. What mattered to her was the fact that I was someone in need. In spite of her meager resources, she took me into her home, her family, and her heart. I shall never forget her. I was so happy for her when I heard that a professor at the college who had recently lost his wife had sometime later asked her to marry him, and she accepted. The loving kindness that she had shown to others for so long was now being returned to her.

After I had stayed with Mrs. George for a year, I heard about another Adventist rooming house where many former students from Oakwood College were staying. I longed for the opportunity to be around my former schoolmates, so I asked the landlady if she had room for one more. She did, and I moved there in 1959. The couple who owned the rooming house were Johnnie and Esther Logan. Mr. Logan was a somewhat shy man who drove a cab for a living. Esther, on the other hand, was a gregarious schoolteacher who thoroughly enjoyed being around people. She was also an excellent cook. All of the roomers did their own cooking, but on Friday evenings, Mrs. Logan would bring us all together for a delicious traditional meal that consisted of fried fish, coleslaw, potato salad, baked beans, and cornbread. It was so delicious, and we looked forward to it each week.

There were four bedrooms on the second floor. Mr. and Mrs. Logan slept in one of them, and the female roomers occupied the other three. The male roomers occupied the basement apartment, which was fully finished and furnished. It had a kitchen, bathroom, and a really big dormitory-style bedroom with a bed in each corner, a desk, and several dressers. It was a comfortable place to live, and the rent was only $35 a month. There was always someone around in the evenings, so things never got boring. Over a period of time, each of the roomers found careers in other cities or moved into their own homes or apartments, and I was the only one left. For a while, this made me and the Logans more like a family than landlords and tenant.

Things were going well for me at the printing office. My income allowed me to buy a used car, which greatly increased my mobility. Going to work every day was something I looked forward to doing. Most people looked forward to the weekends when they could get away from work, but I looked forward to Mondays so I could get back to work.

Military Service:
God Uses the Army to Open Up Whole New Worlds for Me

Every year or so, the printing office would bring in a new batch of apprentices for training. Those trainees became replacements for the older workers who would soon be retiring. My training program was interrupted for two years when I got drafted into the army in 1960. Fortunately, the printing office agreed to hold my job until I got out of the service, at which time I would be plugged into whichever class was in its third year of training. My going into the army meant that there would be a two-year delay in reaching journeyman status and in reaching the top salary, but Uncle Sam was not deterred by those petty concerns of mine.

Please don't think that this interruption of my training was a bad thing. On the contrary, it opened up a whole new world that I probably never would have discovered on my own. God has a way of bringing something good out of what appears to be an unfortunate situation.

All young men in America are required to register with the Selective Service Department on or before their eighteenth birthday. I wasn't aware of that requirement until I was almost a year past the deadline. I was not aware beforehand that there could be severe penalties for failure to comply with this requirement, so I was relieved when the department accepted my honest excuse. It was fortunate that I did register late because it put me later in the rotation of those who were being drafted.

I wasn't drafted until I was about 25 years old. By then I had spent three wonderful years at Oakwood College or in its environs and had been established in my government job for two years. If I had been drafted sooner, none of those things would have happened. God's timing is impeccable. Far from being an unwelcomed interruption in my life, the draft brought me many new and wonderful experiences that could only have come along at that precise time. Now that I've seen the big picture, I no longer view such precision timing as being a mere coincidence. I can clearly see it as God's direct involvement in my life. Do you think that God had anything to do with the timing of these events? I know I do. I could never have planned things so well and achieved such a glorious outcome by myself, *but God* could.

Two of my favorite words in the English language are the words, "but God." No matter what is said before those two words, whether good or bad, those words dramatically change the outcome. To illustrate my point, I will start a few sentences and let you finish them based on what you know about my life: I was born in the ghetto to an unwed mother and was destined to a life of poverty, but God .... I lived in an orphanage for two years, and then for the next 16 years, I was bounced around from one foster home to another, but God .... I had to drop out of college and was about to become homeless because of it, but God .... Are you beginning now to see why those two words are some of my favorites? God makes the difference every time. Any time you see or hear those words, you know that something momentous has happened or is about to happen. It could either be in the form of a special blessing or in the form of God's judgment. No matter what has happened previously, things will never be the same once those words have been uttered. God's involvement in any situation makes a dramatic difference in the outcome.

Mrs. Logan drove me to the Selective Service Office where I was to begin my military service. We hugged and said our goodbyes, and she wept as we parted. She was no longer just my landlady. She was more like a mother to me. Soon I and several others were put on a bus and sent off to Fort Holabird in Baltimore, Maryland, for initial processing. There they gave us a physical examination to see if we were healthy enough to be in the army. Then we and a bunch of others were put on an airplane and flown to Fort Jackson in Columbia, South Carolina, where we joined hundreds of other draftees and were issued our uniforms. After a few days, we were separated into many small groups, and each group was sent to a different place around the country where each group was to receive its basic training. I was put on a train with my group and sent to Fort Sam Houston in San Antonio, Texas. Since I was a conscientious objector (i.e., a person who, for religious reasons, doesn't use weapons), I would be trained to be a medic at the Brook Army Medical Center. So many Seventh-Day Adventists were sent there for training that the army assigned an Adventist chaplain to the base to minister to them and tend to their special needs. Adventist trainees were all given Saturday off so they could observe the Sabbath. The Adventist Church had purchased a house in a beautiful part of San Antonio and converted it into a dormitory. Adventist servicemen who wanted to get away from the military base could go there on the weekends or during their vacation time. I believe that out-of-town family members and friends who were visiting the servicemen could stay there as well. A middle-aged or older Adventist couple operated the dormitory and did everything they could to make our visits there pleasant and enjoyable. They even provided meals every Saturday afternoon. Here again was another example of God's hand in anticipating and providing for the needs of his people.

After three months of very rigorous basic training followed by three months of intensive medical training, we were separated and groups of us were sent off to our various duty stations. My group was sent first to Fort Dix in Trenton, New Jersey, to spend several days there waiting for a ship to take us to Germany.

Our time at Fort Dix included a weekend. We Adventists were greatly dismayed when we saw that the duty roster required us to do KP (kitchen duty) on Saturday, our Sabbath day.

We tried to get the duty sergeant to change our day of duty to Sunday so we could have Sabbath off, but he refused our request. We would have refused duty on the Sabbath and been put in the brig for our refusal to obey orders, but God made that unnecessary. For such a time as this, the Lord had in place at that base an army captain who was not only a personal friend of mine but also the brother of my girlfriend at that time. My friend was Captain Donald Walker. When I told him of our dilemma, he said he would see what he could do. He was off duty for the day and was dressed in civilian clothes when he went to the duty sergeant to see if the duty roster could be changed to accommodate us. When we entered the sergeant's office, he was leaning back in his chair with his feet up on his desk. "What can I do for you folks?" he asked. Donald told him that we would like to have the duty roster changed so the Adventists could have the day off and go to church. The sergeant refused. Donald reached into his wallet and pulled out his military identification card that identified him as a captain, showed it to the sergeant, and said words to this effect, "You don't understand. I'm Captain Donald Walker. I'm not asking you if you want to change the duty roster. I'm ordering you to do so." When the sergeant realized that Donald was a captain, he was so startled that he quickly took his feet off the desk, stood at attention, and saluted as he said, "Yes, sir." The matter was resolved in an instant. We had a marvelous day that Sabbath as we worshipped at the small Adventist church in Trenton. Did Donald just happen to be there, or did God place him there at that particular time and for our benefit? We were in dire straits, "but God" delivered us.

When we said our farewells to Captain Walker, he told us that if we should have any Sabbath observance problems on board the troop ship that we should go to the chaplain about it. It turned out that we would need to follow that advice less than a week later. The ship we were on was the USNS Patch. Its transatlantic voyage would take seven days to complete. That meant we would spend at least one Sabbath at sea. There were numerous troops aboard the ship (I'm guessing there were thousands of them). Among them were about 10 to 15 Adventists. We had become friends during our medical training at Fort Sam Houston. In our spare time we came together to talk and discuss our future assignments in Germany. Among our group was Siegfried Neumann, a native-born German who had become an American citizen. The rest of us had been fortunate to get assignments in Germany, but I believe that Siegfried used his connections and pulled some strings to get his assignment to Germany. I guess he said that if he had to go in the army, he might as well enjoy it in his native country. During the seven days we were at sea, he was kind enough to teach us some basic German words and phrases so we would be able to communicate in a limited way. It was very helpful and laid the foundation that later enabled me to gain greater fluency in the language. I'm not saying that God put him on the ship just for my benefit (although it is a distinct possibility), "but God" did use him to bless me.

At about the middle of the voyage, a small group of us Adventists went to the chaplain to see if we could have Saturday off and if we could use the chapel on that day for worship services. He hesitated at first and seemed to be a bit reluctant. He was not an Adventist chaplain, so he didn't understand our special needs and he seemed unwilling to give us any special treatment. At that point, I told him that if we didn't get the day off we were prepared to go to the brig rather than violate our consciences. When he saw that we were serious, he left us in his office while he went to speak to one of the senior officers. One fellow in our group thought I had gone too far in expressing a willingness to go to the brig. While I couldn't speak for everyone, I was quite serious for myself. When the chaplain came back, he had good news. He cheerfully told us that we could have the day off on Saturday and that we could use the chapel for our worship services. A short time later, we heard an announcement over the ship's public address system that Seventh-day Adventists would be having church services in the chapel at 9:00 a.m. on Saturday, and any other personnel who were not on duty were invited to join them. It's truly amazing how the Lord opened doors for us wherever we were.

Our ship docked at the port city of Bremerhaven, and we were sent our separate ways to various cities in Germany. I was sent to an army barracks called Ludwig's Kaserne in Darmstadt. I immediately went to my first sergeant and explained my need to have Saturdays off. The sergeant was familiar with Adventists and was apparently impressed by them. My request was granted immediately, and for the 18 months I was stationed there, I had no problem observing the Sabbath. I was given a pass every Saturday so I could leave the base and go to the small local church in Darmstadt or to the much larger church in nearby Frankfurt or to any other church of my choosing. Germany's excellent train service made it possible for me to get around with ease as did other modes of public transportation in the cities. Once again, the Lord had smoothed the way for me.

When I went to the small German church in Darmstadt that first Sabbath morning, I still did not know the German language very well, but I was determined to be among God's people anyway. Unlike the English language, the letters in the German alphabet are so consistently pronounced the same way in every word that once I learned the sounds of each letter, I was able to pronounce every word correctly as I sang from the hymn book along with the congregation. My pronunciation was so accurate that those standing next to me thought I could speak German until I explained that I couldn't, but I was steadily gaining greater fluency. Being immersed in German society helped improve my language skills considerably. I loved the language so much that I pursued it with the same enthusiasm I had when I pursued a knowledge of the printing business.

On my first day at that small church, I met another German who had lived for a while in America and was now in the American army. He, of course, spoke fluent English, and we became good friends. His name was Werner Nietsche. He introduced me to his wife, Christa, and they invited me to their home that day and many days thereafter. I learned that his wife was a surgeon. Not to be outdone, he later went to medical school himself after he was discharged from the army. He became an excellent surgeon and was very much in demand for his services at one of the leading hospitals in Frankfurt, Germany.

I was assigned to a dispensary on my base along with several other medics: Milton Crossim, Norman Givens, Clifford Pelham, Stefano Gilona, Private Gifford, and Sergeant Massey. We assisted Dr. Mario Reda in treating the sick and injured. We also gave periodic immunizations. I could not have asked for a better assignment. All of the other troops on our base had to take turns working in the kitchen, but a fringe benefit of being a medic is that we were exempted from that task. We had to be available if our services were needed. We were also exempted from guard duty, which would have required us to stay up all night patrolling various parts of our military base.

Once a year, the Adventist servicemen from all over Germany held a retreat in the Bavarian Alps. The site was located high up on one of the snow-capped mountains at a place that was formerly called "The Eagle's Nest." It had been Hitler's private vacation spot when he was in power, and it was lavishly designed and had grand views of the surrounding mountain peaks. The scenery was absolutely breathtaking in its beauty. Those of us who attended the retreat had much to do and enjoy. There were inspiring guest speakers, great music, sightseeing tours, skiing, rides on special carts deep underground in the salt mines, and much more. In addition, we enjoyed exquisite dining. It was truly an unforgettable experience.

I took advantage of the fact that Germany is located right in the center of Europe. I used my vacation time to travel to many of the major countries in Western Europe, including England, Holland, Belgium, France, Italy, Austria, Switzerland, and others. I had a marvelous time in my travels. It was an experience I would not have had if I had not been drafted, something that would not have happened later with the all-volunteer army. Was it just a lucky coincidence? I think not. I see a heavenly Father continuing to pour out his blessings on me just as he promised he would do for those who are faithful in paying their tithes. It's just another piece of evidence that God keeps his word. I thank God for the timing of my military service and everything else in my life. I developed such a love for Europe that my future wife and I would later spend a full year touring 24 different countries in both Eastern and Western Europe.

Courtship and Marriage

I returned from Germany and was discharged from the service in June of 1962. Instead of going back to work right away, I decided to take a couple of months to relax and readjust to life in America. My room at Mrs. Logan's house was still available, so I settled in there once again. When I returned to the Logan household, I was introduced to Clara Feaster, a former Oakwood College student who was renting a room on the top floor. A few weeks later, her sister came down from Buffalo, New York to visit her. The sister was Wilma Feaster, and she was studying to be a schoolteacher. She was attractive and very vivacious.

Wilma did not know anything about me and was hesitant when I asked if I could take her out. She didn't give me an immediate answer. It was only later after private encouragement from her sister that she agreed to go with me, and thus our relationship began. Most of us assume that two people meeting like that is something that just happens by chance, but I believe it was orchestrated in heaven. The confluence of so many events is too much for me to ascribe them to chance. There's the matter of my discharge and my decision to delay going back to work, Clara's choice of the Logan household as a temporary residence, and Wilma's decision to visit, all of which occurred at the same time. It required a tremendous amount of coordination. If you doubt that heavenly intervention of this sort occurs, read in the Bible the story of Isaac and Rebekah, Philip and the eunuch, Paul and Ananias, and Peter and Cornelius. The story of those divinely arranged meetings can be found in Genesis 24, Acts 10, Acts 9, and Acts 8.

After a couple of weeks, Wilma returned to Buffalo to complete her education, but I did not forget her or how much I enjoyed her company. I returned to work at the Government Printing Office and joined the class that was in its third year of training. There was a great group of guys in that class. It was a pleasure working with them, and many of us became good friends. The office was a great place to work. Not only were there great coworkers, but great bosses, great working conditions, great pay, and other great benefits such as sick leave, vacation leave, and an excellent retirement program. The office also had a superb location. It was situated just a block away from both a commuter train station and a subway stop. City buses passed the office on two streets, stopping right beside the building on each street. From where I lived, it was also an easy commute by car, so there were many ways to get to work. It was the perfect job in the perfect location, and I thrived there. "Made in heaven" is not only a good way to describe it, but probably an accurate one as well.

In the meantime, Wilma completed her education in Buffalo, New York, and moved to Washington, DC, where she immediately found a job as an elementary school teacher. I continued to pursue her, and soon we were an exclusive couple. We were friends with several other dating couples, many of whom had been my classmates at Oakwood. The women in this group of friends began to complain about having to prepare a meal for their boyfriends every Saturday (Sabbath). The men hadn't asked them to do this, but it had become something of a tradition among us. In order to give the ladies a break from that routine, we formed a group called "The Gourmet Society." On the second Saturday of each month, one of the women would prepare a complete meal for the entire group and host the dinner at her home. Not only did it give the off-duty women a break on that day each month, but we had great fun being together and socializing. Each month, we would rotate the group dinner to a different person's home. So after she served her meal, each hostess had six or seven months off before they had to do it again.

Not only did the Gourmet Society come together for the monthly dinner, but we went to social events together, and some of us even traveled together on our vacations. As the couples got married one after another, we were in each other's weddings. The group was so popular that many other couples joined it over the years. So great was the camaraderie among the members that the group is still in existence after 50 years. All of the charter members were single when they joined the group, and now many of them are grandparents.

Early in 1965, I proposed to Wilma, and she agreed to become my wife. Plans were made for our wedding in late August of that same year. We would be married in her hometown of Buffalo, New York. Her mother, whom I consider to be a saint, worked at Roswell Hospital, but she was also a highly skilled seamstress. She made the wedding dress and, with the help of some seamstress friends, made a lot of the dresses for the bridesmaids. She also organized a group of women at the church to prepare a delicious meal for the reception, which was held in a large annex attached to the church. Hundreds of friends, relatives, and church members attended the ceremony, which turned out to be a beautiful and memorable event.

Since Buffalo is very near to the Canadian border, we spent our wedding night at a motel close to Niagara Falls. The next morning, we went up to the very edge of the falls to get a close-up look at that awesome and mighty force of nature. While we were there, we took a ride on a boat called the "Maid of the Mist." After all of the passengers put on raincoats and rain hats, the boat took us through the roiling waters at the bottom of Niagara Falls. I don't remember whether the captain took the boat through the falls or around them, but somehow he got us behind the falls to a relatively calm area in a large cavern that can't be seen from the outside. Most people view the falls from the top. From there, you would never be able to see the cavern. Later we toured the beautiful flower gardens surrounding the falls, then we left and headed for New York City. The World's Fair was being held there that year, and we wanted to spend a couple of days taking in all of the activities and sights at the fair. Next, we took off for our ultimate honeymoon destination in the area of the Pocono Mountains in Pennsylvania. We lounged at the pool, did target practice with a bow and arrows, went on romantic strolls, and took in the awesome beauty of the Poconos. That is truly one of the most beautiful regions in the country, and it's easy to see why it is a major honeymoon spot for so many newlyweds.

After the excitement of that week, it was time for both of us to get back to work. We settled into a brand-new apartment in the Maryland suburbs around Washington, DC. When I say that it was a brand-new apartment, I mean that literally. The builders had just completed construction on the huge, sprawling apartment complex called Pleasant House Apartments, and we were the very first occupants of our apartment. When I returned to work, my coworkers welcomed me back and presented me with a brand new set of cookware as a wedding present. The people of the office were more than just coworkers to me. They had become like an extended family.

At the end of every day, a typewritten copy of the speeches, decisions, and other actions in the Senate and House of Representatives on that day is sent to the Government Printing Office (GPO). Overnight, the GPO has to print and deliver bound copies of the Congressional Record to the office of every senator and congressman by seven or eight o'clock the next morning. That is the primary mission of the GPO. In order to fulfill that mission, the office has to operate 24 hours a day. The office needed typesetters and proofreaders to work at night. In order to avoid making some workers stay on night duty permanently, small groups of employees would take turns working nights for two or three months. At the end of that time, they would return to the day shift, and another group would be sent to work nights for the same amount of time. Those groups were not voluntary. At some point, everybody had to take a turn working nights. That arrangement was fair to everyone, but it posed a real dilemma for me. If I were to work the night shift, I would have to work Friday nights. The Sabbath day begins at sunset on Friday and ends at sunset on Saturday. The entire first half of the Sabbath day is on Friday night. If the office insisted that I take a turn working nights, I would have to resign the job I loved so much because I love God more.

I decided to ask my supervisor if I could be excused from night work. To my surprise, he said that the decision was not his to make. It was up to my coworkers and the union that represented them. They would discuss the matter and then vote on whether to exempt me or not. When the time came to discuss and vote on the matter, I was asked to step out of the room and await the decision. My future was in the hands of 25 to 30 coworkers, or so it seemed. Of course, as with my entire life, my future was in God's hands. Minutes passed slowly as I waited. What would they decide? After about 15 minutes, I was called back into the room where smiling faces told me that my exemption had been approved. It was such a great relief.

Once again, God's hand and favor were upon me. He intervened and resolved the matter so quickly that my life went on without any interruption. Having read my story thus far, you must be as amazed as I am at the consistent pattern that has emerged. Every time a problem arises or threatens to arise, God swiftly moves in with a solution without any major effort on my part. It is comforting to know that we can depend on God to get us through any situation, no matter how bleak and hopeless it seems.

A few years later, an opportunity for a promotion came to my attention. Most of the upper level jobs were located on the eighth floor. Since the jobs required a knowledge of the printing business, the office recruited from among the craftsmen in the pressroom, the bookbindery, and the typesetting departments. I was hesitant to apply, but Wilma encouraged me to do so. God used that nudge from my wife to open up new and wonderful vistas for me. A few weeks after I took a test for one of the available positions, I was notified that I had been accepted. This resulted in a substantial increase in pay and new opportunities for advancement. God had said that he would pour out so many blessings on the faithful and obedient that they would not be able to receive them all. This promotion was further evidence that God keeps his promises.

For my new position, I was assigned to a desk in one of the offices on the top floor where most of the administrative offices are located, and I was given the title of printing specialist. I and about 30 other promotees were put through an intensive training program to learn our new duties. We were now a part of the Printing Procurement Department, and our duties would be to make arrangements with private printing companies to do the printing of various government publications and forms. We ordered extra copies of selected government publications and we sold those to the public. The agencies also paid us for the printing that we did and/or for our contracting services. By these means, we made enough money to cover all of our operating expenses. Not only did it not cost the government and taxpayers anything to fund the Government Printing Office, but we prided ourselves on being the only government agency that made a profit, which was given to the Treasury Department every year.

All government departments and agencies are required to send all of their printing needs to the GPO to be printed. The volume of work that is received is so great that the GPO can print only about 20 percent of it. The remaining 80 percent is made available to private printing companies all over the country. Those companies compete with each other by submitting bids for a chance to produce the vast amount of work that is available.

In my new job, I and others in my department had to write contract specifications describing the requirements for each job that was put up for bids. After the printers submitted their bids on or before the specified date, the bids would be opened publicly. Awarding of the contract was not automatically made to the lowest bidder. My job required me to certify that the lowest bidder was capable of doing the work in accordance with our quality requirements. This sometimes meant that I or someone from our quality control department had to visit the contractor's place of business and look at his equipment, his plant operations, and samples of his work.

Once we had chosen a winner and made the award, I had to monitor the contract to make sure it was performed satisfactorily and on time. If there were any complaints by the customer agency, I had to investigate and resolve them. I was assigned 30 to 35 different contracts for which I was responsible each year. I loved my new job, and I thrived in it. The new job was both challenging and rewarding for me. God will never place you in a situation that you cannot handle without providing help and training for it, so don't be afraid to try new things. If God puts you in a new or unfamiliar situation, it's because he knows you have the capability to learn, grow, and increase your capabilities in that new environment. In the process, you will discover that you had capabilities of which you were not aware. When a door of opportunity opens for you, go boldly through it with complete trust in God.

Things were going well for Wilma and me both in our marriage and in our careers. Then came the sad news that Wilma's mother had died after a long battle with stomach cancer. Wilma and her sister immediately set about making arrangements for her funeral even as they mourned her loss.

I would like to pay a special tribute to Wilma's mother. Mrs. Feaster was a truly remarkable woman. When her two daughters were quite small, her husband abandoned her, leaving her to fend for herself and raise the girls on her own. Instead of bemoaning her situation, she made the best of it. She worked hard to earn a living. In the meantime, she raised her daughters to be self-reliant and independent young adults who could take care of themselves whether they had a husband or not. She committed herself to provide a college education for the girls. After she had accomplished that goal, she went back to school herself, and I believe that this enabled her to substantially increase her income. So wisely did she manage her income over the years that she was able to purchase three two-story houses which, after being divided up into separate apartments, provided a total of seven rental units. These rental units provided her with additional income. Always thinking of her daughters, her will stipulated that the properties and everything she owned would be passed on to them upon her demise.

Further evidence of Mrs. Feaster's love for her children and of her self-sacrificing nature was demonstrated when her daughter Clara got married. At the time, Clara's husband was about to enter graduate school, and Clara had not yet begun her career, so they didn't have much money. They desperately needed a car, but couldn't afford one. Mrs. Feaster thought they needed a car more than she did, and so she gave them her car. I believe she went without a car for a while. In order to be completely fair to both girls, she gave Wilma the cash value of the car that she had given to Clara.

Mrs. Feaster's thrift, her hard work, and her devotion to God blessed our lives tremendously and provided us with a splendid example of how we should live our lives. While flawlessly performing all of the many activities in her life, she very ably served the church as superintendent of the Sabbath school department. She was well loved and respected by all of the church members. After the well-attended funeral service, it was with heavy hearts and a great sense of loss that Wilma and I returned to our duties in Washington.

Our European Adventure:
God Enables Us to Fulfill Our Dreams—He'll Do the Same for You

Early in 1969, I was telling Wilma how much I had enjoyed my time in Europe and how much I would like to go back. She said how much she had wanted to visit Europe, and so we began making plans to go. We didn't just plan for a vacation of two to four weeks. We stunned everyone when we announced that we were going to quit our jobs and spend an entire year traveling in Europe. I know that sounds strange the way I've been going on and on about how much I loved my job, but the lure of Europe was something I could not explain, and I now believe that God had some very wonderful experiences in mind that he knew Wilma and I would enjoy. However, if I did not have faith and a willingness to go on this adventure, none of those experiences would have been mine. I tried unsuccessfully to get a leave of absence for a year. I was told that I could not get a leave of absence for that amount of time unless it served the needs of the office in some way. When that effort failed, I asked my supervisor what she thought of my chances of being rehired if I resigned for a year, and she thought they were pretty good. On the strength of her reassurance, I moved ahead with my travel plans.

By this time, we had saved about $12,000, which was a lot of money in those days. It would be more than enough to finance the entire trip. When we were traveling through Europe, we didn't carry cash with us. We used American Express Travelers checks, which were accepted the same as cash in all of the countries we visited. By doing that, we had the reassurance of knowing that we could get our money back if the checks were lost or stolen.

We made all of our travel arrangements through the American Automobile Association (AAA). I was amazed at the wide range of services that were available through AAA. They booked passage for us on a French ocean liner, the S.S. France. They arranged for us to purchase a Volkswagen camping bus and to pick it up in Amsterdam, Holland. We chose to pick up the Volkswagen in Holland even though we were going to spend the first two weeks in England. We wanted to avoid the confusion of driving on the left side of the street in England and then having to adjust to driving on the right two weeks later when we crossed over to the European continent. AAA also arranged for our vehicle to have international license plates and insurance. They provided us with guidebooks and road maps for all of Europe. Their guidebooks helped us to determine what sights we wanted to see and helped us to plan our itinerary.

Since we were going to stay at campgrounds throughout most of our time in Europe, AAA provided us with a complete guidebook to all of the campgrounds in Europe. Since great numbers of Europeans stay in camps when they travel, the campgrounds were always first rate. They were in beautiful park-like settings. Many of them had toilet facilities, showers, lakes or swimming pools, recreation areas, laundromats, convenience stores, and many other amenities. The beautiful part of the camping experience was that you could stay in the camps for $3 to $5 a night.

Another thing that I learned from AAA is the fact that there are American Express offices in all of the major cities in Europe. Those offices provide a free mailbox service and may be used as a temporary mailing address to receive mail. If we knew we were going to be in a particular city at a certain time, we could have our mail sent there and held for us to pick up. We used that service many times, but one occasion stands out in particular. When we were traveling through Denmark, Norway, Sweden, and Finland, we decided that we wanted to go into Russia as well. Unlike most countries that give you a visa on the spot as you cross over their border, Russia required two weeks to process a visa application, and they asked where they should send the visa if it was approved. We knew we would be in Helsinki, Finland, before we entered Russia, so we told them to send it to the American Express office in Helsinki. We eagerly checked the mailbox day after day, knowing that if we didn't receive it within two weeks we would have to abandon our plans to see Russia. On the last day before our deadline, the visa arrived. It gave us great peace of mind to know that we could count on American Express for that service.

AAA thought of everything, and their assistance helped to make our trip a thoroughly enjoyable experience. However, one of our favorite guidebooks did not come from AAA. We bought it at a bookstore, and it proved to be invaluable to us. It was written by Arthur Frommer, and it was called *Europe on Five Dollars a Day*. He listed numerous "bed-and-breakfast" accommodations and restaurants that literally enabled one to see Europe on five dollars a day.

We had never before planned a major trip like this one, so we learned what to do as we went along. All of the elaborate preparation I just described for you are things we had never done before. I learned something valuable from that experience. What I learned is that on a human level there is nothing more powerful than a person who has made up his mind to do something, commits himself to do it, and follows through on it by taking the necessary action. Commitment followed by action is an act of faith, and God always responds to faith. Once you make the commitment, God follows through by bringing to your attention the things you need to know and by providing the means to accomplish your goals. Nothing great is ever accomplished without faith and commitment followed by decisive action. To those three attributes, I would add one more: persistence. Once you have an idea or a dream that you believe is worth pursuing and have committed yourself to accomplish it by taking the necessary action, you will have to be persistent in your efforts. Let neither discouragement, laziness, or any other apparent obstacle dissuade you from accomplishing your goal. Apply those four principles (faith, commitment, action, and persistence) to everything you undertake, and you will find yourself achieving one success after another. All four steps are necessary if one is to accomplish anything or have any kind of success in life.

With all arrangements made and our bags packed, we set sail on May 19, 1969. We knew not what adventures awaited us, but we were eager to find out. Shortly after we got settled in our cabin, a steward knocked on our door and handed us a bottle of champagne. Our travel agent at AAA had sent it as a way of thanking us for all of the business we had brought him. He had no doubt received a sizeable commission on it. We don't drink, but we appreciated the gesture. We poured the champagne down the drain and kept the bottle as a souvenir.

There were so many activities on board the ship that we could hardly keep up with them all. There was a gym, a swimming pool, table games indoors and outdoor games on the deck. In the evening, there were different shows featuring singers, comedians, and live bands. There was also dancing for those who were so inclined. My favorite activity was to sit in the sun on the deck and look at the vast amounts of water as far as one could see in all directions. I especially enjoyed watching the seagulls and other birds that apparently rode aboard the ship all the way across the Atlantic. We were too far from land for them to have flown that far out to sea every day. Every time the ship's crew dumped the garbage into the ocean day after day, the birds would fly down from the ship in huge numbers and feed on it.

The ship stopped briefly at the city of Le Havre in France to discharge a few French passengers. We were told that the ship would be there for several hours before it continued its voyage to England. We were free to leave the ship if we wanted to walk around the city. Wilma and I decided to do that and take in some of the sights in that port city. It was around noon when we finished our self-guided walking tour and decided to find a restaurant and have lunch. When we found one, the waiter greeted us courteously and handed us a menu. With only a rudimentary knowledge of French, I couldn't read the menu, but when I saw the words "steak tartare," I figured I couldn't go wrong with steak, so I ordered it. I had no idea what steak tartare was. To my horror, it turned out to be raw steak with a raw egg on top of it. There was no way in the world I was going to eat that! Since it was my mistake, I paid for it and left. As I was leaving, I believe I saw the waiter give it to another patron who was delighted to have a free lunch. I learned a very valuable lesson that day. Know what you're ordering. Don't guess about it. Have someone translate it for you.

After a few hours, we sailed off to Brighton, a seaport city at the south of England. We boarded a train there and soon found ourselves in the sprawling, bustling city of London where we would spend the next two weeks. We had a marvelous time taking in the major sights in London, including the royal residence at Buckingham Palace; Westminster Abbey where the coronation ceremonies for kings and queens are held; the Tower of London where the crown jewels are on display and guarded by the famous beefeater guards;

Windsor Castle; the Houses of Parliament with Big Ben, the gigantic clock that chimes every hour; and Trafalgar Square with its statue of Lord Nelson who defeated Napoleon at Waterloo. We also rode on London's bright red double-decker buses and its famous subway, which is usually referred to as "the tube." We strolled along the Thames River, watched the ceremonious changing of the guards at Buckingham Palace, and listened to the various speakers in Hyde Park as they defended their views on different topics or criticized the view of others.

We were fortunate enough to be at a public place where Princess Anne was scheduled to make a speech. We got there ahead of time and joined the crowd that was awaiting her arrival. I positioned myself where I had a good view of the speaker's podium, and I held my camera up to my eye to make sure I could get some good pictures of her. I told my wife that I thought I could get a good shot of her. A policeman standing nearby quickly turned around and stared long and hard at me. Apparently the word "shot" meant something different to him than what I intended. He saw that my intent was harmless, and he relaxed again. A more zealous officer might have hustled me away to be searched and questioned. In a foreign country, one has to choose words carefully.

There were many other sights that we saw in London, but one of the things that we enjoyed the most was visiting the Adventist churches there. On our first weekend, we visited one church and enjoyed the services very much. After church, one of the older members invited us to his home for dinner and conversation. He and his wife were wonderful people and made us feel very welcome in their home. One of the questions I asked our host was how do Englanders put up with the frequent rain showers that fall there. He said they simply ignore it. If they paid any attention to it, they would never get anything done. His was a very pragmatic view of things.

On the next weekend, we went to a different church, and we were warmly received there as well. A young couple, Mike and Helma Kellawan, invited us home for dinner. It turned out that he was the youth leader at the church. He invited us to return to the church that afternoon for the young people's meeting and asked if we would agree to be interviewed at the meeting and answer questions about life in America. We agreed to do so. The questions from the interviewer and the audience showed that they had a fair understanding of Americans, but one question surprised me. The interviewer said that he had heard that America was becoming a matriarchal or female-dominated society, and he wanted to know if it was true. I told him that I had not observed any such shift in American society. In hindsight, I should have said that there is a move toward equality but not dominance. We became very good friends with the Kellawans, and we remained in touch long after we left England. They even came to visit us when we were living in Germany, and Mike came to visit us after we returned to the United States. Our experience in England was typical of what would happen everywhere we went in Europe. Church members were continually inviting us home for dinner, and we made many friends that way.

Soon it was time for us to leave jolly old England and take the ferry across the English Channel to Holland. After the boat pulled away from England's coast, Wilma went off on her own. I believe she was trying to find a restroom. I waited for her on deck. I and scores of other passengers stood at the rail watching the coast of England as it faded in the distance or at the wave below as our boat cut a path through it. Before long, an attractive young Dutch woman joined me at the rail and started up a conversation with me. I'm not sure what her intentions were, but I thought it best to let her know right away that I was married. I told her I wanted her to meet my wife who was soon to return. She seemed surprised and a bit disappointed when I told her that I was married, but she stayed there to meet Wilma when she returned. The three of us found seats and talked together for the remainder of the ride. We found out that she lived with her father, and every few months or years she went to a different foreign country and stayed long enough to become fluent in the language of that country before returning home to stay briefly with her father again. She was just returning from one such trip to England or some other country. I'm not quite sure what her reason was for learning all of those languages. She must have had some goal in mind. Before we parted, she gave us her name and phone number. She told us to call her if we wanted her to give us a guided tour of Amsterdam.

We did call her, and we had a wonderful time being escorted by our personal tour guide. She took us to some of the major sights around the city; then she took us to a place that we probably would not have chosen on our own. She took us to the famous (or infamous) "Red Light District." Our guide felt that this area was such a major part of life in Amsterdam that we had to see it. What we saw was hard to believe. There was a section of town with numerous storefronts with huge plate glass windows. Behind those windows sat one or more women advertising their availability by displaying a red light bulb that was shining brightly. I'm guessing that if only the white light bulb was shining, it meant that the woman was available but currently busy with another customer. When neither bulb was turned on, it meant that the madam was not available. With this system, men can literally go "window shopping" for the woman he wants to be with. To us, it was a shocking example of moral depravity, but the Hollanders seemed to be unashamed of it. In fact, they seemed to be proud of the "civilized" manner in which they have handled the business of prostitution.

God usually had shielded us from exposure to things like the "Red Light District." Why had he allowed me and Wilma to be brought there and to see it for ourselves? God always has a purpose for the things we experience in life. Perhaps it was to keep us from being naïve or unaware of what happens to a society when it turns away from God and his commandments. Someone famously said, "What one generation tolerates, the next generation embraces." Whenever one generation fails to take a stand against sin, the next generation grows up exposed to that sin all their lives and they think there is nothing wrong with it. What are some examples of this principle in the history of mankind? There are several that come to mind, but there are many more besides these. God had said that we should flee from fornication. One generation of Hollanders said, "What's the harm in prostitution? It takes place between two consenting adults and no one is being harmed by it." God had been pushed out of their thinking, and it no longer mattered what he said on the subject. What that generation of Hollanders began to tolerate, the next generation embraced and took to a whole new level. Having grown up in that kind of permissive society, succeeding generations of Hollanders see nothing wrong with it. In fact, they seem to take pride in showing it to tourists as a model of how it should be done.

Other examples of the principle at work in our lives are as follows: God said that our bodies are the temple of God and that we should not do anything to harm them or alter them. One generation of Hollanders decided that using narcotic drugs was not so bad, and so they legalized it. The next generation embraced it to the point that young people in Holland began using those substances openly in public and walking around completely stoned. It got so bad that young people could be seen passed out on the street or on a park bench with a hypodermic needle stuck in the arm. Those young people will end up making no positive contribution to society all because the previous generation tolerated the use of narcotic substances. God said, "Thou shalt not kill." One generation tolerated the killing of unborn babies. The next generation embraced the practice so much that they passed laws permitting it. Abortion mills sprang up everywhere, and thousands of babies are killed every year. There are very few these days who see the harm in it or the damage that it does to society. God said that marriage was the union of a man and a woman. One generation decided that it didn't matter what God had said, and that we could define a marriage any way we wanted. God said that the Sabbath day was the seventh day of the week. When man changed the Sabbath day from Saturday to Sunday, one generation tolerated the change in God's law, and succeeding generations embraced the change so thoroughly that most people are not even aware that an unauthorized change has been made. They are not aware that Saturday and not Sunday is the Sabbath chosen by God and enshrined in the ten commandment law. Few people seem to have learned the lessons history has taught us. History has shown that nations that adhere to the laws of God tend to prosper, while those that reject his laws go into decline. All too frequently these days, we hear news reports of additional aspects of God's law that have been rejected by Americans. I fear for our future if we continue down that path. When one generation tolerates sin in its midst, the next generation sees it as normal, and they embrace it fully.

After seeing the best and the worst of Holland, we were ready to see the rest of Europe. We picked up our Volkswagen camping bus and drove to a nearby campground where we rented a spot among the others who were camping there. We took time to get familiar with our bus, which had sleeping space for two people plus one more when the top was pushed up. It also had a sink, an icebox, a closet, vast amounts of storage space under the seat and elsewhere in the vehicle, and a seating capacity for seven people. We went to a camping supply store where we bought a propane gas cooking stove and a chemical toilet, and we were all set to explore Europe.

Our year-long tour took us to 24 different countries. We saw all of the major cities and had a marvelous time in all of them. What follows is just a small sampling of the things we saw and did during our travels. In France, we saw the city of Paris from atop the Eiffel Tower, enjoyed the artwork displayed at the Louvre Museum, visited the beaches along the French Riviera, and toured the palace at Versailles and the Notre Dame Cathedral with its magnificent stained glass windows. There is so much ancient architecture in Italy that the whole country is like one big museum. While there, we climbed the stairs to the top of the Leaning Tower of Pisa, strolled through the ancient coliseum in Rome, visited the Vatican, rode a gondola through the canals of Venice, viewed Michelangelo's awe-inspiring artwork on the ceiling of the Sistine Chapel and his magnificent sculptures, including the Pieta (a statue of the Virgin Mary weeping as she holds the crucified body of her son Jesus on her lap) and the grand statue of King David. We also saw Leonardo da Vinci's famous painting of the Last Supper of Jesus with his disciples. In Switzerland, we rode cable cars to the top of the Matterhorn and the Jungfrau, two of the tallest mountains in the Alpine mountain range. We enjoyed Switzerland's forested countryside and its gorgeous lakes, including Lake Lucerne and Lake Geneva. In my opinion, Switzerland has the best natural beauty in all of Europe, and possibly in all of the world.

God found yet another way to bless us during our travels in Europe. We didn't plan it this way, but we were fortunate to be in Zurich, Switzerland, in 1969 when the Adventist church held its worldwide youth congress there. Thousands of Adventist young people from all over the world gathered there for a week-long assembly. We desperately wanted to attend the meetings, but since we hadn't known about them ahead of time, we were not registered as delegates. Consequently, we could not attend the meetings. Determined to find a way to go to the meetings, we went to the organizers of the conference and appealed to them to let us go to the meetings. They were sympathetic toward us and said that if we would help them set up the tables and chairs and perform other tasks to help them get the building ready that they would give us admission cards and meal tickets. We were ecstatic and eagerly accepted the offer. Now we would be able to attend the meetings and have meals with the delegates.

The meetings were thrilling. We were all equipped with headsets so we could hear translations of the many foreign languages spoken by the various speakers. We sang, prayed, and worshipped together. We also listened to inspiring sermons and heard reports about the work of the church in various countries around the world.

Guided by An Unseen Hand

Outside on the parking lot, there were hundreds of buses that brought people to the meetings. We just happened to be on the parking lot when the bus arrived bringing delegates from Buffalo, New York, and Wilma got a chance to see and greet a lot of friends from her hometown. We also made many new friends from all over Europe, and we later visited some of them in their homes when we continued our travels throughout Europe. We could never have planned what turned out to be such a spontaneously exciting and enjoyable week, but God could and did. All we had to do was to follow King Solomon's advice: Acknowledge God in all of our ways and trust that he would guide our paths and our choices. It is evident from the wonderful way in which things were going that he was indeed guiding our path. There is one more happy footnote to that week in Zurich. We had been out of touch with world events during that week, so we were not aware that America had landed a man on the moon. The citizens of Switzerland were so excited about the news that one of them (a total stranger to us) rushed up to us on the street when he saw that we were Americans and excitedly asked us if we had heard the news. Looking back on that wonderful week, I am just amazed at how much God was involved in arranging for our happiness and enjoyment of life.

In Spain, we saw a bullfight for the first time. It was quite a spectacle with a lot of very colorful ceremony. Elegantly-dressed matadors skillfully and agilely tempt the bull and then evade its charge time after time. When an unlucky matador gets struck, picadors rush out to distract the bull until the downed matador can be carried away. A successful matador ends the fight with a single thrust of the sword downward into the bull's heart. As an award for his accomplishment, he is given the ears of the bull as a prize. The bull's carcass is sent away to provide food for the poor and homeless. Spain's Prado Museum in Madrid contains some of the finest artwork in the world. In Russia, we visited the sprawling area known as Red Square. There we saw the massive red marble buildings, one of which contained the still-preserved body of Vladimir Lenin. We also saw St. Basil's Cathedral with its numerous and very colorful onion-shaped domes.

We thoroughly enjoyed staying in the camps in most of those countries and meeting like-minded travelers. We had all of the amenities we needed for a tiny fraction of the cost of a hotel room. At one of the camps in France, we went for a swim in the lake. Wilma wanted to go out to the middle of the lake, and she started wading out in that direction. Suddenly, the bottom dropped away from under her feet, and she started to go down. I was about ten feet away from her, and my back was toward her, so I didn't know this was happening. With no fear or panic in her voice, she calmly and quietly said the word "help." She said it only one time, and she said it in her normal speaking voice. I turned around and saw that she was in trouble. I quickly swam over to her, put my arm around her waist, and got her to safety. I asked her why she didn't scream and yell for help. She said she knew I would come for her. She was right, of course, and it was good to know that she had such complete confidence in me.

We decided not to travel during the wintertime, so we rented an apartment in Germany for several months. The place we chose with the help of a real estate agent was a lovely upstairs apartment in a two-family house. It was located in a small village in the Taunus Mountains a few miles north of Frankfurt, Germany. The city was called Schmitten-im-Taunus. We could easily commute to the big city of Frankfurt for most of our major activities and then retreat to our little mountain hideaway.

One of the things we wanted to do that winter was to brush up on our language skills. So we enrolled in a German language class at the Berlitz Language School in Frankfurt. Five days a week, we were in class all morning long, and we made considerable progress in developing fluency with the language.

We made many friends among our classmates, most of whom were foreigners from other countries who had come to live in Germany just as we had done.

Ever the socialite, my wife invited the entire class to our apartment for lunch one day. We all crowded into our apartment, and everyone had a good time eating and trying to find a common language in which we could talk. Somehow we made ourselves understood. Friendship is its own language, and very few words are necessary. One of our classmates was a Muslim from Egypt. He told us that it was Ramadan, a month-long Muslim holiday during which Muslims do not eat or drink anything until after sunset each day. Even though he was unable to eat with us, he still enjoyed the opportunity to socialize with us outside of the classroom. We had never heard of Ramadan before. If we had known, we would have scheduled the dinner for another time. Being aware of cultural differences is a constant challenge when traveling abroad. A good guidebook can be invaluable in that regard.

Each weekend, we went to the large Adventist Church in Frankfurt. On our first Sabbath there, I was surprised and delighted to see a German friend I had met when I was stationed in Germany eight years earlier. His name was Lothar Furch, and he was an engineer at Germany's equivalent to General Electric. We were overjoyed to see each other again, and we agreed that Wilma and I would come to his apartment for supper with his wife and daughter every Thursday evening. Those wonderful evenings together provided them with an opportunity to practice their English and allowed us to practice our German.

My reunion with Lothar after so many years may have been a chance occurrence, but I don't think so. I think it was prearranged before I came back to Germany, and I see divine fingerprints all over it.

By the first of March, winter had begun to loosen its grip on the European continent, so we gave up our cozy apartment and resumed our travels. We headed southward toward warmer places like Greece and Turkey where we would spend a few weeks until spring fully arrived on the rest of the continent. When we were in Zurich, Switzerland, at the worldwide Adventist Youth Congress the previous year, we had met a couple who were stationed at a U.S. Air Force base at Incorlik, Turkey. They had said we should come and visit them sometime, and we thought this would be the perfect time to do so. We spent two weeks with them while we waited for springtime to arrive.

When we first crossed into Turkey, we were fully stocked with food except perhaps for meat and dairy products. For some unknown reason, we decided to live mainly on the foods we had with us. We did buy fruits and vegetables that we found in the small marketplaces, but we didn't buy any milk or meat. When we got to the home of our friends, they asked us if we had drunk any milk or eaten any beef since being in Turkey. When we indicated that we hadn't, they said that it was good that we hadn't. They informed us that there was quite a bit of tuberculosis among the cattle. We didn't know about it, but God did. Once again, his guiding hand was with us and kept us from a very real danger that could have ruined the rest of our trip and possibly the rest of our lives. At the time, we took it for granted and didn't give God any special praise. We may have said, "Thank God," but that was about the extent of it. God deserves more praise than that when he helps us avoid a catastrophe. Now, however, when I look back on God's involvement in my entire life, that incident elicits special thanksgiving and praise. There are those who might say I was just lucky, but when you put this incident together with all of the others in my life, you have to know that there is more than just luck at work in my life. It is none other than the hand of God.

While we were driving through Turkey one day, we stopped by a stream and used water from the stream to wash our vehicle. While we were doing that, an elementary school teacher dressed in a suit and tie approached us. We didn't speak each other's language but we were able to communicate quite well in German. He was very friendly and told us that he was on his lunch break. The school at which he taught was just a few yards away, and he invited us to come and meet his students. They were a lively bunch of children, and their interest in the foreigners was short-lived. They wanted to get back to their fun and games before recess was over. After introducing us to the students and making a few remarks, he took us to his nearby house where his gracious wife welcomed us and served us some light refreshments. We chatted for the remainder of his lunch break, and then we had to be on our way. We got his address and wrote to him briefly after we returned to America. They were such a charming couple that I would have liked to know them better.

If we had been at that stream an hour earlier or an hour later, we would have missed the opportunity to meet the teacher and his wife. God's timing is impeccable. Knowing that our life and times are in God's hands allows us to live lives relatively free from anxiety. We can live knowing that a loving Father has many wonderful things and experiences in store for us just as he has done in the past.

Most of our travels in Europe went off without any kind of trouble, but we did have a few problems. Once when we were in Madrid, Spain, we parked the car in what seemed to be a valid parking place and went off sightseeing on foot. We were gone about 45 minutes, and when we returned, we were horrified to see a policeman having our vehicle hooked up to a tow truck. We rushed over to him and asked him to stop. When he saw that we were tourists who had made a mistake and not some local scofflaw, he smiled, made a few friendly remarks, and ordered our vehicle to be released. We breathed a huge sigh of relief. If we had been just five minutes later, our vehicle would have been gone and we would have had no idea where it was. Except for the things we had put in storage, everything we owned was in that vehicle. Was it merely fortunate timing on our part or God's prompting that caused us to return to our vehicle when we did? At the time, we were just so happy to have our vehicle that we didn't give it much thought, but now that I look back at the consistent pattern of God's involvement in our lives, there is no doubt that it was he who brought us back at just the right time. The Lord knew how devastated we would have been if we had lost our vehicle in a foreign country, and he prompted us to return to it when we did. Those things are not to be taken for granted. Praise be to God!

Another potential problem occurred while we were traveling in Hungary. We parked our vehicle one night, closed the curtains, and went to sleep. When we woke up in the morning, we discovered that both rear tires were flat. We could have dealt with one flat tire by using the spare, but two flat tires at the same time presented us with a serious dilemma. How do you deal with something like that in a foreign country where you don't speak the language? How do you even begin to explain the situation and ask for help? We knocked on the door of a nearby factory. The door was opened by a security guard. When I asked him if he spoke English, he indicated that he did not. When I asked if he spoke German, he said "*ja*" (yes), but he hated to speak it because of what the Germans had done to his country in World War II. Nevertheless, he agreed to do so since German was our only common language. When I showed him the two flat tires, the good-natured guard took over the situation. He called a repair shop that sent us a mechanic. While the mechanic worked on the problem, the guard and I engaged in friendly conversation. He introduced us to factory workers as they arrived for work. I believe he even offered us some fruit or something he was eating as a snack.

In the meantime, the mechanic encountered a problem that we had not anticipated. Back in those days, the country of Hungary lagged far behind the rest of the world in technology, and they didn't have the capability to fix tubeless tires, which is what we had on our vehicle. What were we to do now? The clever mechanic solved the problem by stuffing old-fashioned inner tubes inside our tires and inflating them. It wasn't a perfect solution, but it worked and we were soon on our way.

Was it a coincidence that we were parked in front of that particular facility? Was it pure luck that this particular guard was on duty and was able to help us? I fully believe that God was involved in delivering us from an impossible situation. When I look back at my entire life and see the big picture, I stand amazed at all that God has done.

Another incident occurred while we were traveling in Russia. When we checked into our hotel in Moscow, the desk clerk was supposed to tell us that a short distance from the hotel there was a special guarded parking lot that we were supposed to use. There were a lot of people checking in at the same time. The clerk was overwhelmed and forgot to tell us about the special parking lot, so we parked our car on the street right below our hotel window. That way, we could keep an eye on it during the day and we would hear the alarm if anyone tried to enter it during the night. No one attempted to enter our vehicle, but when we went out to it in the morning, we discovered that someone had stolen our rear license plate and the antenna. It was only petty thievery, but it created a major problem for us. I couldn't drive around without a license plate on the rear. I reported the matter to the hotel staff. They apologized for not telling me about the guarded parking lot, and they called for the police to come over and investigate. The police officer could do nothing to replace the license plate, but he typed a letter that explained our situation and authorized us to drive without a license plate. We were to show that letter if we were stopped by the police. We did have to use that letter or my explanation of it a couple of times when we were stopped by police.

As fast as problems arose during our travels, solutions followed immediately. We were never terribly inconvenienced by anything. This pattern repeated itself wherever we went. I could ascribe all of that to pure luck, but I think I'd have to be willfully blind and ungrateful not to see God's involvement in all of it. All too often, we take these things for granted. As we live our lives, we get so caught up in our day-to-day activities that we fail to see the beautiful mosaic that God is creating. Often it is only when we see the entirety of our lives that the picture becomes clear. Only then will we realize the full extent of God's involvement in our lives.

When we first left America for Europe, we knew that Germany would be our home base in Europe. So we went to Germany shortly after our arrival on the continent and put most of our money in a German bank. When we opened the account, the bank officer asked us if we wanted the account to be in American dollars or in German marks. Since we were going to be in Europe for a whole year (most of it in Germany), we chose German marks. It turned out to have been a very good choice (not because of any brilliance on our part, but due to divine providence). During the time that we were in Europe, the federal government decided to take America off of the gold standard. Because of that decision, American currency was greatly devalued compared to other currencies. When we were ready to return to America, we closed our account and took a check payable to us in American dollars. Our German marks were worth so much more than the newly devalued dollars that we made quite a lot of money when we made the exchange. It's almost as if God was working overtime to find ways to bless and prosper us. I know nothing about currency trading, so I'm convinced that it was God who prompted us to open that account in German marks. He found yet another way to pour out the blessings that he promises to those who faithfully pay their tithes and offerings to him. There are those who would call it a lucky experience, but I don't. Now that I look back on my entire life, I'm able to see what others cannot.

In May of 1970, we concluded our travels in Europe and sailed once again across the Atlantic Ocean on the same French ship that had taken us to Europe a year earlier. Our camping bus was stored in the ship's cargo hold and traveled with us. Once you've driven such a versatile vehicle, you want to hold onto it. We would use it for years as our principal means of transportation and for camping trips.

When we arrived in New York City, we drove first to nearby Teaneck, New Jersey, to visit with Thaddeus Wilson and his family. He was a good friend as well as the minister who had performed our wedding ceremony five years earlier. We were delighted to see each other, and we laughed and talked for several days as we brought each other up to date on our lives. The days we spent with them gave us time to acclimate ourselves to life in America and to a seven-hour time difference. At that time, I was 33 years old and Wilma was 29. When Pastor Wilson realized how old we were, he was only half joking and half serious when he told us that we needed to get busy making babies. I knew he was right. All of our friends who were the same age as we were had children who were five or six years old.

Before we could start a family, I had to find work and a place to stay. For that, we headed back to the Washington, DC, area. When I applied for my former position at the Government Printing Office, I was told that there were no openings at that level. However, a job was available at my previous position as a typesetter. For some reason, which I can't explain, I just didn't want to go back to working at the trade even though it was a good job and the salary was excellent. For reasons unknown to me, I turned the position down and decided to go back to college and complete my education, which had been interrupted years earlier. I know now that the decision was influenced by the hand of God because so many wonderful and necessary experiences lay ahead of me.

Returning to College to Complete Some Unfinished Business

We decided that I would go to the University of New York at Buffalo. To minimize expenses, we would occupy one of the apartments left to us by Wilma's mother. We could stay there rent free. (It wasn't totally rent-free. In fairness to her sister who would lose her half of the rental income on the apartment, Wilma paid her one half of the former rental rate.)

Wilma was happy with the choice because she would be back in her hometown and among old friends for a while. Being drafted into the army years earlier had proved to be a blessing to me when it brought me many wonderful experiences and opened up all of Europe for me. Being drafted into the army was about to be a blessing to me once again. Because of my military service, I was eligible for the GI Bill, which would pay for much of my education. In every conceivable way, God was pouring out his blessings on me. Once again, God had foreseen my future needs and made provision for them without any planning or effort on my part. He also provided me with a part-time job at the university library, which helped a lot with our expenses. Looking back on it, I'm not even sure how I became aware that the job was available. Somehow, God brought it to my attention without any real job search effort on my part. I needed it, and God supplied it.

Another unexpected way in which God supplied our needs was through something called "gleaning." There were many commercial farms around Buffalo. After the farmers had sent the harvesting machines and workers through the fields, the public was allowed to come into the fields and glean what the harvesters had missed. We got huge quantities of food in that way, some of which could be canned or frozen. I believe the food was free. If we did have to pay, the price was so low that it might as well have been free. I still remember Wilma making grape juice from concord grapes that we obtained by gleaning.

Parenthood: Our First Child Is Born

Even though I was in school and money was tight, we could not put off starting our family. The old biological clock waits for no man, and ours was ticking down. Wilma became pregnant late in 1970. We immediately started taking Lamaze classes in natural childbirth (we wanted our children to be born without Wilma taking any anesthetics, epidurals, or pain medication because we did not want the baby to be affected by these things). Babies born by natural childbirth are more alert and inquisitive at the moment of birth than the others are. We found that to be true in our case. Even while the doctor was holding our daughter upside down, she was turning her head from side to side as if she was trying to focus on all of the people and activity in the delivery room. We also planned to breastfeed our children, and the Lamaze class taught us how to do that. We had heard that breastfed babies have higher IQs than bottle-fed babies and they score at least one letter grade higher than the others. From my observations, these statistics also appear to be accurate. Both of our children were reading with a high degree of proficiency at age four and were able to skip a grade in elementary school. My daughter graduated from college as valedictorian with the highest grade point average in a class of 800 graduates. Both of my children went on to earn master's degrees. That's only anecdotal evidence, but I am certain that natural childbirth and breastfeeding were factors in their academic success. It's interesting to see that doing things God's way always produces the best outcome. I'm so glad that Lamaze was available to us. They made an invaluable contribution to the well-being of our children.

Because of my Lamaze training, I was prepared to be in the delivery room when my daughter was born. I knew what to expect at each stage of delivery. Wilma had been trained by Lamaze about the different stages of labor, what to expect in each stage, and special techniques of distraction and rapid breathing as natural ways to minimize pain. I was amazed at our daughter's alertness and curiosity right at the moment of birth. While the nurses cleaned up our daughter, Wilma was taken to a private recovery room, and I joined her there. A short time later, a nurse brought our daughter to us and placed her in my arms. I looked into her eyes and smiled at her, and she smiled at me. It was a very special moment for me that I shall never forget. When I told friends about it later, they discounted my story. They said that newborn babies don't know how to smile. They attributed it to gas, but I know that there was a connection between us when our eyes made contact, and that her smile was real and intentional.

Wilma's mother's first name was Clara and her middle name was Etta. In honor of her mother, Wilma combined the two names into one and named our daughter Claretta. I hope my daughter realizes the great honor that was bestowed on her with that name.

My wife and newborn daughter remained in the hospital for several days. When I left the hospital that first day, I was filled with such joy and emotion that I felt as if I were walking on a cloud. I was so excited that I just had to tell someone the good news. Wilma's mother had a good friend named Anne Harley. This dear old lady had become a close friend of our entire family. She lived just a few blocks down the street from the hospital, so I went to her house and shared the news of our daughter's birth. Afterwards, I spent the next two or three days thoroughly cleaning the house and setting up the furniture in the baby's room. In those few days, I felt driven to remove every speck of dirt and to have everything ready for my wife and baby's arrival. (I believe that my obsession with cleaning the house is a fairly common phenomenon called "the nesting instinct" and is akin to a bird preparing its nest.)

When the children were weaned from breast milk, we had to decide what kind of milk we would give them. We decided not to give them whole milk, which contains huge quantities of fat. The large amount of fat in cow's milk is designed to nourish a baby cow, which weights 80 to 100 pounds at birth. That amount of fat is good for a calf, but it is far too much for an infant child. Consequently, our children never had any problems with childhood obesity or any of its associated problems.

The recommendation to use 2% milk was made by the children's pediatrician, and I am glad that we heeded his advice. God's guidance often comes to us through people who are more knowledgeable than we, but we should never consider it to be a mere chance occurrence or a bit of good luck when that happens. Instead, we should recognize it for what it really is: evidence of God's involvement in our lives and of his ceaseless efforts to enhance and enrich our lives. The fascinating thing to me is that such knowledge rarely comes too soon or too late, but almost always at the moment when needed. Having seen the pattern repeated over and over, I have come to the point that I confidently expect it. That can be your experience, too.

God's guiding hand was evident in the way we chose to feed our children when they were infants and as they grew older. During the first few months of their lives, the children were fed exclusively on breast milk with an occasional sip of water. Wilma took a doctor-recommended vitamin supplement to ensure that her milk would meet the nutritional needs of the children.

Let me just interject this important bit of information at this point. If a woman intends to breast feed her baby, she most tell her doctor well in advance of her delivery date and must keep reminding him throughout her pregnancy. Doctors almost routinely come into the delivery room prepared to give mothers an injection to prevent them from lactating (producing milk). Doctors do that almost automatically because the vast majority of women choose not to breast feed, but to bottle feed their babies. Those women choose convenience over God's preferred method of feeding our babies. Mother's milk is specifically designed by God to meet the needs of newborns. No formula that comes in a bottle can match the formula designed by our creator.

If a doctor approaches a woman with a hypodermic needle in his hand, whether it happens in the delivery room or at any point during her time in the hospital, she should ask him what it is for to make sure that he doesn't inadvertently thwart a woman's intention to breast feed. Wilma even refused injections for pain, knowing that it would have an undesirable effect on the baby. It was a sacrifice that she willingly made for the benefit of the babies, knowing that any pain killers she took would diminish their alertness at birth and possibly have other negative effects later on. It is a good idea to remind your doctor of your intentions in this regard all during your pregnancy and while in the hospital. Make sure that the hospital staff is aware of it, too. If a woman is fortunate enough to have her husband in the delivery room, he can keep the doctors and staff informed of her decision regarding breast feeding and pain medications. The more natural the child birth, the more it aligns with God's intent.

When the children were ready for solid food, we decided that we would not feed them with commercially available baby food. We made that decision because we could not be certain if those foods had been cooked at high temperatures for a prolonged period of time (such cooking is destructive to many nutrients and enzymes). We also could not be certain of how much exposure to oxygen had occurred during processing (prolonged oxygen exposure is also destructive to vital nutrients). Finally, we could not be certain of how long those foods had remained in warehouses and on grocery store shelves before being purchased (time has a detrimental effect on packaged goods, which is why they have expiration dates). We wanted our children to receive all of the nutrients that God had put into those foods without any loss or damage being done during processing.

I feel certain that God guided us in the decisions we made in regard to how we would feed our infant children after they were weaned from breast milk. See if you think that what we did happened by chance or if God's guiding hand was involved. At a baby supply store, we discovered a device that enabled us to convert the same freshly-cooked vegetables that we adults ate into a puree that the babies could eat. It was a small hand-cranked device. We put the solid food into a small hopper on top of the device, turned the crank handle a few times, and voilé! Out at the bottom came instant baby food. A small amount of water could be added to further soften the food, but that usually wasn't necessary. Today there are small blenders that can do the same thing or something similar. We didn't let them eat between meals, so they always had a good appetite at meal times, and there was no burping or throwing up because of partially-digested food being mixed with a between meal snack. We also chose not to give our children any refined white sugar. If any sweetener was deemed necessary, we used only honey or raw, unrefined brown sugar in small amounts.

Another fascinating discovery that we made on our own was that many raw, soft fruits required no processing at all. Citrus fruits, of course, could be squeezed for the juice. Soft raw fruits such as apples, pears, peaches, bananas, and many others could be converted into instant baby food by simply taking the tip of a teaspoon and lightly scraping the soft fruit. The scrapings provided instant baby food with all of the enzymes and nutrients intact and undamaged. One of the children's favorites was dried apricots, which we got at a health food store. We soaked them overnight to soften them, and then pureed them in a blender. We and the children enjoyed that natural treat. The same thing can be done with raisins.

Except on rare occasions, we did not allow our children to eat candy or other sugary confections. Healthful treats can be made or bought at health food stores. We found a more healthful way to satisfy their sweet tooth. Cookies, pies, and other pastries were made at home from freshly-ground whole wheat flour. We chose to stay away from refined white-flour products, and we used only whole grain breads, cereals, pancakes, waffles, and pastas. To make sure the flour was fresh with no rancidity and none of the wheat germ and other nutrients removed by refining, we purchased whole-grain wheat kernels at the health food store and made our own fresh whole wheat flour using a superb tabletop grinding mill that we bought from a grain company in Nebraska, I believe. It could be adjusted to provide the desired degree of fineness or coarseness without exposing it to high heat. Wilma provided many wholesome treats for the family. Among our family's favorite treats were

Wilma's homemade cookies and sweet potato pie with a whole wheat crust. We did use store-bought whole-grain breads and cereals.

Our efforts to give the children the very best possible nutrition paid huge dividends. Our children had excellent health with very few illnesses. They excelled in school and were accepted into an advance placement program in high school. They excelled in college and did well in their careers. I feel certain that we were guided by God in these matters because we had no special training along these lines other than the guidance taught by the Adventist Church. However, we went way beyond those teachings into totally new territory. We simply acted intuitively as we felt impressed.

Wilma and I had decided ahead of time that she would not work after the birth of our children—at least, not until they were all in school. The only exception to that decision was to hold a few Tupperware or Coppercraft sales parties in the evenings or on the weekends when I was home to take care of the children. God saw that we were sincere in our commitment to our children, and he found a way for Wilma to hold down a full-time job and still honor that commitment. The Adventist Church in Buffalo, New York, had established a Christian elementary school. The church board knew of Wilma's qualifications as an educator, and they asked her if she would serve as the school's principal. Knowing of her decision to stay at home with our two-month-old daughter, they allowed Wilma to set up a playpen in the principal's office and bring the baby to school (the baby slept most of the time, so there was very little distraction from Wilma's duties as principal). That was a very generous accommodation by the board that served everyone's interests. It was another demonstration of God's provision for our needs in the most unexpected ways. We didn't seek this opportunity. It sought us. People usually go looking for a job, but how often does a job come looking for a specific person? It's simply too much to be a coincidence. Once again, the hand of God was leading us in totally unexpected ways and in places we had never even imagined. Our God is truly amazing! If you haven't already done so, give your life to him and let him run it. He'll do a far better job than you ever could on your own.

A Trans-Canadian Journey to Alaska

When my classes were over for the summer of 1972, Wilma and I decided to do some traveling. The Canadian border was only 30 minutes or so from where we lived. We planned to start our trip in Ontario, Canada, and drive westward along the Trans-Canadian Highway all the way to the west coast. We would stop at various sights along the way. I was astounded at how long Lake Superior is. We started at one end and drove for hours. Every time we looked to our left, it was still there. It took almost a whole day of driving to get to the other end of it. As we continued driving westward, we eagerly looked forward to visiting Norman and Gerda Liske on their huge farm. They lived in Canada, but Gerda had grown up in Germany, and we had met them in Germany when they were visiting Gerda's relatives. All during their visit to Germany, Gerda had been speaking in German with her relatives, and poor Norman understood not a word of it. He was bored out of his mind the whole time. When he saw us at church in Frankfurt and realized that we spoke English, he was so excited. He latched onto us and stayed with us. He was so thrilled to finally have someone with whom he could speak English. We invited them along with some other church members to our apartment in Schmitten for dinner and an afternoon of conversation in English. I believe it was the highlight of his vacation. We had remained friends and kept in touch over the years. We had a wonderful reunion with them in Canada and introduced them to our daughter. Norman was in his element on the farm. He was up before dawn milking the cows or planting and harvesting crops. He loved all of it—and best of all, everyone there spoke English.

After we left the Liskes' farm, we continued traveling westward through the remaining provinces, passing beautiful Lake Emma and the castle in that area. We finally reached British Columbia on the west coast. The awesome natural beauty of that province reminds me of Switzerland with its many snowcapped mountains and gorgeous lakes. It was there that I saw huge quantities of totem poles, which were vivid reminders of the region's Eskimo and Indian heritage.

Next, we drove our camping bus up through the Northwest Territory until we reached the beginning of the Alaska Highway, which was also called the "Alcan Highway" because it connects Alaska and Canada. In those days, the Alaska Highway was an unpaved gravel-and-dirt road, so it was 1,000 miles of rough driving conditions. Fortunately, there were very few cars on that road, but every time a car did pass you in either direction, you had to contend with huge clouds of dust obscuring your vision or bits of gravel striking your vehicle. When it rained, you had to deal with mud and the possibility of skidding on it. The stones kicked up by passing cars could crack your windshield, break a headlight, or nick the paint on the car.

It has been my frequent observation over the years that when you commit yourself to do something, God moves to bring to your attention the things you need to accomplish your goal. We had a friend in Buffalo named Nathaniel Wilson who was a younger brother of the minister who married us. Nat had traveled the Alcan before, and when he learned of our plans to do so, he gave us all sorts of good advice. He told us how to put a screen over the windshield and the front of the vehicle to protect it from flying stones. He also gave us clear plastic covers that we could put over the headlights to protect them. Now, you could say that it was just a coincidence that Nat happened to be in Buffalo at the time, learned of our plans to travel on the Alcan, had previously traveled there as well, and had retained those plastic headlight covers all those years later and was willing to give them to us. You could say that all of those things were mere coincidences, but you would be missing the very wonderful way in which God involves himself in our everyday lives. Please don't take these things for granted. We did initially, but now we know better.

Along with us on the trip, we took Michael Gayle, the 12-year-old son of a lifelong friend of Wilma. He was excited to be with us on this trip and was fascinated by the many sights we saw along the way. Additional space could be created in the bus when the top was pushed up. It was up there that Michael slept in a stretcher that could be unfolded to make a bed. The seats in the back of the bus folded down to make a large bed, and it was there that I and my family slept. It was very ingenious the way Volkswagen put so many things in such a small space.

We stayed in some of the camps and state parks along the route to Alaska. At one camp, we discovered a thermal spring in which people were luxuriating. We donned our bathing suits and joined them in the soothingly warm water. It was as good as being in a spa, and it was free. At one campground, Michael went off on his own to explore what the camp had to offer. A few minutes later, he came running back to us and excitedly told us that he had seen a bear. We were in a camp full of people, and no one else had said anything about seeing a bear. Somewhat disbelieving, we went with him to see for ourselves. Sure enough, there was a little bear cub running around the camp. The cub was obviously very used to being around people. It showed neither fear nor hostility and appeared to be in a playful mood while it looked for anyone who would give it some food. We knew that where there were cubs, a protective mother is not far away, so we stayed close to the bus just in case she showed up and was not quite as friendly as her cub.

After seeing the bear, we stayed in the camping bus after dark just to be safe. Needless to say, I was quite annoyed when Wilma woke me up once in the middle of the night and asked me to accompany her to the outhouse. I understand that she couldn't use our chemical toilet because Michael was in the vehicle, but still I was not too eager to go outside if bears might be around. She insisted that it was urgent, so I grudgingly strapped on my hunting knife and grabbed my flashlight. Anxiously we made our way to the outhouse. I stood guard outside while she went in. A few seconds later, I heard her announce from within that it was a false alarm. It turns out that she didn't have to go as much as she had thought. We both laughed. I jokingly scolded her on the way back to our vehicle. I said, "You got me up in the middle of the night and put my life in danger for a few drops of urine!" I think she was truly embarrassed herself, but at least she knew that I would stand by her no matter what the danger.

When we reached Alaska with its paved roads, we were relieved to finally be off that long and dusty Alcan Highway. We were also relieved to find that there was a camp at the end of the highway, and its best feature was a huge area available for motorists to wash the large amounts of dust and mud from their vehicles. I believe the Alcan has since been paved, so motorists traveling to Alaska today should not encounter any dust or the other hazards we faced.

On our own, we toured the major cities of Alaska (Fairbanks, Anchorage, and others), and then we went on a guided tour to see the natural beauty of Alaska's wilderness and mountain areas. We were thrilled to see the famous Dahl sheep that live and frolic way up near the top of some of Alaska's highest mountains. They have the uncanny ability to safely leap from one narrow ledge to another without falling off. They seem to be totally fearless and to have supreme confidence in their abilities. It made me nervous just to watch them. One misstep could have sent them tumbling down the mountainside, but it never happened. It's amazing to see how well God has equipped each kind of animal for its particular environment. It's awe-inspiring to see the wide diversity of animals; the rich beauty of so many flowers, trees, and other plants; the grandeur of tall snowcapped mountains; and to enjoy the tranquility of gently flowing rivers, lakes, streams, and waterfalls. What's even more awe-inspiring is the realization that God created all of these things for our enjoyment.

There was one aspect of nature that took us a while to get used to. That was the fact that there were about 22 hours of daylight every day during the summertime. The sun would go down briefly in the middle of the night and then come right back up a short time later. We went to bed at ten o'clock because we knew it was bedtime, but it was still daylight outside. We could hear construction crews working 24 hours a day to take advantage of the extra daylight and the warm summertime weather. When winter came, it would be too cold and too dark for them to work. Fortunately, we were not there during the wintertime when I believe Alaska is in almost total darkness the whole time. On top of that, it's freezing cold all winter. I don't know how Alaskans endure such conditions.

When we were in Anchorage, we visited the Adventist Church there on Sabbath. We thoroughly enjoyed the worship service, and we were pleased to accept an invitation to dinner that was extended to us by Mr. and Mrs. Nash. We enjoyed meeting them and their children and learning about life in Alaska. After a delicious meal, Mr. Nash asked us if we would like to have some moose meat that he had in his freezer. We, of course, said that we would, and so we had our first taste of that rare delicacy. We found it to be rather tasty.

After dinner, Mr. Nash took us for a walk on one of the many glaciers in Alaska. It was truly awesome to see those massive sheets of ice. I believe it was somewhere around this time that our daughter celebrated her first birthday.

When we left Alaska, we stopped in Tacoma, Washington to visit Wilma's sister whose husband was pastor of one of the Adventist churches there. After the rigors of Alaska and the Alcan Highway, it was nice to be back on paved roads and back where night and day occurred at normal intervals every 24 hours. It was also nice to be with close family again. It was on this occasion that Wilma announced to them and to me as well that she might be pregnant with our second child. That generated a lot of excitement and gave us something to which we could look forward.

After we said farewell to our relatives in Washington, we chose a route that took us through some of the most scenic regions of the country. We marveled at the size, beauty, and grandeur of the Grand Canyon. We visited the Great Salt Lake where we tested its purported ability to keep our bodies afloat without any effort on our part and found that it was true. While we were in Salt Lake City, we visited the Mormon Tabernacle one evening and were fortunate to listen to their famous choir rehearse. It wasn't the same as a formal concert, but to us it was almost as good. Our next major stop was at Mt. Rushmore where we beheld one of the most magnificent pieces of sculpture anywhere in the world. There, carved into the side of the mountain, are the faces of some of our best-known presidents. It's hard to imagine the planning, skill, and hard work that it took to create this masterpiece. It was created by Gutzon Borglum, who figured out how to use dynamite to strategically blast away certain chunks of rock to produce the breathtaking images we see today. It is an awesome sight well worth visiting both in the daytime and at night when the floodlights are trained on it. Seeing it in pictures is not enough to appreciate this grand work of art. Until you are there in person looking up at it, you cannot truly appreciate just how awesome it is. All in all, that summer vacation was one of the best I've ever had. I thank God for putting it in our hearts to undertake this adventure and for blessing us all along the way.

As with Adventist churches everywhere, the church in Buffalo was a very friendly church. The members were so close that they became like a huge extended family. We would visit each other in our homes and go places or do things together as easily as we might do with a close relative. One elderly member of the church was part of a group that was not affiliated with the church. It was a social group that called itself "The Happy Thirty Club." About 40 years earlier, the 30 original members of the club purchased a huge house out in the country. The house sat on 40 acres of land and had its own private lakefront out back. It was a two-story house with a screened-in front porch and numerous bedrooms upstairs and downstairs as well. The members of the club used to go out there and spend their weekends and vacations there together. They were getting older now and weren't using the place very much at all. This elderly church member began inviting us to go out there with her so she and her somewhat frail husband wouldn't be out there alone. We went with them and fell in love with the place. The club was eager to bring in younger members to keep the club going, and they asked us to join. We soon found out that the now-feeble older members were no longer going to the clubhouse at all. It wasn't long before we found that we had the entire clubhouse all to ourselves when we went out there. We would take guests of our own from the church out there on weekends, and before long, one other Adventist couple joined the club. One summer, I painted the kitchen and the entire exterior of the house, and we also put in a vegetable garden out back. It was such a beautiful place to go to and relax, and God had made it available to us absolutely free except for very minimal membership dues.

One summer evening, my family and the other young couple who had joined the club were sitting outside the clubhouse just as the sun was going down. We were enjoying the red glow in the sky as the sun slowly disappeared. Suddenly, we saw a steady stream of bats flying out of the attic through a small hole right where the roof comes to a point at both the front and back of the house. The bats emerged from the opening one at a time in rapid succession. We began counting the number of bats that flew out from both the front and back of the house. By the time the exodus ended, we had counted a total of 378 bats, and that was on top of the hundreds that had already come out when we started counting. The bats had been so quiet during our previous visits to the clubhouse that neither we nor the older club members knew they were up there. They slept all day and were out all night, so nobody had a clue that they were up there until that night when we just happened to be sitting outside at the right time. The house had sat empty for so many years that it was only natural that the bats would choose it as a place where they could nest undisturbed—that is, until we came along.

Coexistence was not an option that we were willing to even consider. We simply would not stay in a house that was occupied by bats. When the last of the bats had come out and gone off into the night to search for insects, I got out the extension ladder and climbed up with a bunch of rags to stuff into their entry and exit holes. We put one car in the front yard and one in the back yard and turned on the headlights to provide illumination. While I was working, Wilma and one other lady climbed up on the roof and waved a broom back and forth in case any bats came back before I finished my work. Thankfully, none did come back while I plugged up those holes. They don't come back and forth to the nest. Apparently, they stay out all night in search of food. Just before sunrise in the morning, the bats returned. They were frustrated and confused to find their usual points of entry blocked. They flew in huge swarms around the house, screeching frantically. Bats have something built into their DNA that compels them to be in a dark place during the day. After a long night of hunting, they were also exhausted and needed to find some safe place to sleep. As the sun started to rise, they finally flew away in a desperate effort to find shelter. Some of them flew into the tool shed we had in the backyard. Others probably flew to barns in the neighborhood. It was such a relief to know they were no longer in our attic.

It's amazing how easy it was to get rid of the bats in just an hour or two. We set our minds to accomplish the task, and God provided an immediate solution. Ours is a partnership that I've come to rely on all of my life. All too often we take credit when things work out so well. I'm reminded of the words of Jesus when he said, "Without me, you can do nothing." I think those words are truer than most of us realize. The apostle Paul adds to that statement by saying, "I can do all things through Christ who strengthens me."

When Jesus said that we could do nothing without him, he was sharing an invaluable truth with us, and it's important that we grasp what he meant. That statement by Jesus is confirmed in many places all throughout the Bible. We are repeatedly cautioned against pride and arrogance. Pride implies that our accomplishments are ours alone and that we achieved them solely by our own efforts. I think the apostle Paul said it best when he was speaking out against pride. Apparently there were some people who were boasting about their accomplishments. He rebuked those prideful people to whom he was speaking when he said, "What do you have that you were not given?" He realized that while we can do nothing without Christ, we can do all things through him when we abide in his will.

While many of the activities previously described in this chapter were occurring, I was continuing my studies at the university. By the summer of 1973, I had completed my studies, and was ready to graduate. My graduation ceremony was attended by a dear friend of the family named Martha Dockery. She had been a longtime close friend of Wilma's mother. We affectionately called her "Ma Dockery." When Wilma's mother died, she volunteered to be a mother to us, and she truly did fill the void for us. She was the tenth woman to fill that role in my life. Most people have only one mother. I was blessed to have ten, each one coming at a critical point in my life.

God Opens the Windows of Heaven and Pours Out Multiple Job Opportunities

I graduated with a bachelor of arts degree in English. It was a degree that would benefit me substantially when I resumed my career as a contract specifications writer at the printing office two years later. With my family growing, I had to find some immediate employment. As soon as the need manifested itself, God immediately became involved as he had done all throughout my life. Without much effort on my part, one job opportunity after another presented itself to me. One of our church members named David Barnes had a contract with Hertz, a car rental company, to go to distant cities and pick up rental cars that had been dropped off and bring them back to their point of origin in Buffalo. A group of us would travel in one of the cars to those distant cities, and we would pick up the waiting cars and drive them back to Buffalo. We did this only on Sundays, so it was an easy way to earn extra money without interfering with our regular jobs during the week. On one occasion, we had to pick up cars in Toronto, Canada. We obtained permission to make an excursion of this assignment. We took our wives along. After we picked up the waiting cars, we did some sightseeing in Toronto and had dinner at a nice restaurant before heading home to Buffalo. To show you God's hand in the matter, I didn't even seek that job. David invited me into it.

Another job opportunity presented itself to me in an unusual way. A family friend who was a plumber did some plumbing work at our house. While he was there, he saw some remodeling work I had done in our home, and he asked if I could remodel the basement of one of his customers. I had never done it professionally, but I said "yes." The woodworking shop that I took way back in junior high school and the skills that I learned elsewhere gave me confidence that I could do it. I had to erect frames for the walls, hang doors on hinges, install wood paneling, put in a suspended ceiling and ceiling lights, and put vinyl tile on the floor. There was an open toilet in the basement, and I had to enclose it to create a private bathroom. I arranged with a licensed electrician to do the wiring and install electrical outlets. The work went very well, and I had a thoroughly satisfied customer. God had seen to it that the experience I had gained in my youth prepared me for what I would do in the future.

On another occasion, a church member wanted to have the interior of her house painted, and I got that job. I had not done any advertising of my skills, so I have no idea how she even thought to ask me if I could do the job. Some might say it was luck or word-of-mouth advertising, but I know in my heart that it was God at work fulfilling his promise to pour out blessings on the faithful.

Wilma attended a class on how to buy property, fix it up, and sell it for a profit (it's a practice called "flipping"). Using the training she acquired in the class, she searched the classified ads looking for foreclosed properties that were being sold at auction. She found a four-unit apartment building and told her teacher about it. We didn't have the money or the experience to bid on it, so she asked the teacher if he could put up the money. (I don't know where she got the nerve to do that, but that's the way she is.) The teacher was a real estate broker who had a $75,000 line of credit at the bank, so he was able to do it. The building was in such a desirable location that the teacher said he could "steal" the idea from Wilma, but he was a man of integrity, and he would put up the money and partner with us. He went to the auction with us, and we observed as he did all of the bidding for us. We got the building at a bargain price, and the deal we made with the teacher was that he would get back all of the money he had used to buy the property when we sold it, and we would split any profit that was made. The strategy was to renovate and upgrade the building to enhance its value when we sold it. I did all of the cleaning, painting, and remodeling of both the interior and exterior of the building. We raised the rent on all of the units to make the building more attractive to prospective buyers. When the work was all done, the building sold immediately to the homeowner who lived right next door. He liked the idea of being close enough to oversee his investment. It turned out to be a win-win situation for all parties concerned. As the psalmist said in Psalm 23, our "cup runneth over." All praise be to God!

After I graduated from college, I looked for more steady work. I went to the Manpower temporary agency to see if they had anything available. They did, and within less than an hour, I had a job. They sent me to Hanover Manufacturers Bank and Trust Company. There I would work as a courier. My duties included running the mailroom and delivering both cash and other items to the branch bank in nearby Tonawanda, New York. The job came with a station wagon that I was allowed to take home with me every day. The job satisfied my need for income and provided me with transportation to work. After I had been on the job for only a short while, the bank decided to make me a permanent employee, working directly for them and not for Manpower. I felt especially honored when I found out that I had been chosen instead of the son of a bank officer who had hoped to give that job to his son when he graduated from high school in a few weeks. Normally, company executives look out for each other in those matters, but God gave me favor with the senior executive officer.

When I came to work every day at the bank, I wore a dress shirt and a necktie. I was friendly and conversant with all of the employees in the bank from the highest executives to those on the bottom rung of the ladder. One rather arrogant bank teller asked me why I wore a necktie to work every day. In so many words, he essentially said that I was, after all, just a lowly courier. In essence, I told him that my job didn't define who I was. Being a courier was something I did to earn a living. It was not who I was on the inside. I dressed to reflect the image I had of myself.

South of the Border, Down Mexico Way

Always on the lookout for jobs that allowed her to be at home with the children during the day and then do sales work in the evenings and on weekends, Wilma started selling Coppercraft products at home parties. After doing that for a while, she began selling Tupperware as well. Then her income and benefits began to skyrocket. Wilma met or exceeded all of her sales goals with Tupperware. She was made a team leader and was given the use of a brand-new station wagon every two or three years. In addition, she won an all expense paid vacation for two to Acapulco, Mexico, where we stayed at the ultra-luxurious Acapulco Princess hotel. We and several hundred other successful salespeople who went with us on a chartered plane were treated to a banquet one evening. We saw all of the wonderful sights around Acapulco. One night as we sat at an outdoor restaurant situated on top of a cliff by the ocean, we watched the famous cliff divers diving nearly a mile into the ocean below. First, they said a prayer and did the sign of the cross before each dive. They knew that if they didn't hit the water in a perfectly vertical manner and part the water cleanly, they wouldn't survive or they would be badly injured. The cliff was so high that each dive seemed to last for several minutes. As we watched, we almost felt like holding our breath until the diver safely hit the water. The suspense was heightened even more when it took almost five minutes for the diver to come back up to the surface of the water. The dive took them so far down into the depths of the ocean that it took that long before they could come back up. We cheered and applauded each time we saw a diver come back up to the surface. Fortunately, there were no mishaps the night we were there. I don't know how they got up the courage to do it the very first time they ever did it, much less how they continued to do it night after night.

Among the other exciting things I did in Acapulco was to get harnessed into a parachute attached to a speedboat. When the boat raced away at high speed, the parachute became airborne, and I glided along about a hundred feet up in the air. The boat took me for miles along the shoreline, and the view from up there was spectacular. After fifteen or twenty minutes, the boat stopped, and I glided down to a soft landing on the beach. I don't believe Wilma had the courage to do that activity. We did go horseback riding on the beach together. Wilma had a gentle horse that walked or trotted at a slow pace. I, however, seemed to have a wild bronco that bolted away at high speed and was out of control as soon as I got on it. I don't know whether the horse did it intentionally or not, but it ran so close along a row of thatch-roofed huts that my arm was scraped quite a bit. I think it was trying to get me off of its back. Once I pulled back firmly on the reins, it settled down and I had an enjoyable ride.

When Sabbath came, we found the address of the local Adventist Church and set out on foot to find it. When we got in the neighborhood of the church and still hadn't found it, we stopped a woman on the street, and in very badly fractured Spanish, we said, "¿Donde est iglesia Adventista?" She eagerly motioned with her hand to indicate that we had to go straight ahead and then turn left at the corner. So friendly and helpful was she that she motioned for us to follow her, and she took us most of the way there and pointed out the building when we were within sight of it. We joined the congregation and had a wonderful time fellowshipping with them even though we didn't understand Spanish. After the service, some of the members were kind enough to invite us to their homes for dinner. We very much appreciated the invitations, but we declined them so we could get back to the hotel. Those are just a few of the wonderful memories we had of our time in Mexico. All of it was the result of Wilma's hard work and the steady outpouring of God's blessings upon us.

After working at the bank for a couple of years, I felt impressed that it was time to get a job that was commensurate with my education and experience. Five years earlier, when I returned from Europe, I applied for a job as a printing specialist at the Government Printing Office, but there were no openings. I decided to apply again to see if anything had changed. I said it before, and I'll say it again: God's timing is impeccable. This time there were seven openings, and the office was having difficulty finding anyone who would take those positions. The reason they could not fill those positions was the fact that unions had obtained so many huge pay raises for people working at the printing trade that they were making more money than printing specialists. The tradesmen would have had to take a pay cut to accept a position as a printing specialist, and of course, no one was willing to do that. This left the seven positions open at the very time my application came in. The office eagerly accepted it, and I was hired immediately. That set of circumstances could have happened by chance, but I don't think so. The pattern has been too consistent and too repetitive to be assigned to chance. What a thrill it has been for me to look back and see how God was so closely involved in my life and how he opened so many doors for me. If one of those positions would have been open when I returned from Europe, I would have taken it, but then I would have missed out on all of the wonderful experiences I had in Buffalo. I am so grateful to the Lord for arranging and scheduling things the way he did. There was no strategy or planning on my part. It was entirely his doing. God knew which path would bring me the greatest amount of enjoyment, and he directed me down that path.

With a job waiting for me at the Government Printing Office, we packed up and moved south to the Maryland suburbs around Washington, DC. I plunged into my career, and Wilma continued working with Tupperware until both of our children were in school.

Wilma's Amazing Parenting Skills

When the children started school, Wilma got a job as a schoolteacher. This worked out beautifully because she had the same schedule and vacations as the children, so we never had to use babysitters. Before the children even started school, Wilma had taught them how to read. She had given them a great head start, so naturally they excelled when they went to school.

God seems to have blessed Wilma with extraordinary parenting gifts, skills, and instincts. She seemed to know just what to do at every stage of their development. When they were infants, the only nourishment they got for the first six months was breast milk and small amounts of water. Consequently, there was no gas, colic, nasal congestion, or frequent burping. We did not engage in baby talk with the children. We spoke to them in full and complete sentences, just as we would to any other person. Consequently, they didn't have to unlearn anything; they could go directly to the development of proper language skills. To facilitate the learning process, I would hold our infant children in my arms and read aloud to them anything I happened to be reading at any given time, whether it was the Bible, a newspaper, or a magazine. Of course they couldn't understand any of it, but they were continually hearing the rhythms and patterns of adult speech. We limited the amount of time with each session so as not to overstimulate them. When they were less than a year old and considerably less than two, they already had some clear and advanced speech capabilities. I remember one occasion when our daughter was still a babe in arms. We took her to church, and all of the church members came over to see her. One woman came over and started talking to our daughter, not really expecting the baby to reply. The woman waved her hand and said "hi." Our infant daughter responded by saying "hi." The woman was so startled that she jumped backward and walked away shaking her head in amazement. As she walked away, I heard her say, "Now that's scary."

I cannot say enough about what a fantastic wife and mother Wilma is. Her ability to plan ahead is a gift that was of great benefit to our family. Among the many things that Wilma had to do were the following: Plan and prepare meals and clean up afterwards, keep the house clean and do the laundry, and make sure the children's needs were met and that they got to school and other activities on time. On top of all that, she held down a full-time job (this list is certainly less than half of all the things she did on a daily basis). She coordinated and handled all of those things and more, and she did it so effortlessly that she was never stressed. She actually made it look easy. I still ask myself how she did it all. Our lives were truly blessed because of her gifts of organization and time management.

Wilma's ability to do long-range strategic planning was truly phenomenal. In fact, it is that unusual ability that determined the birth dates of our two children. When we decided that we were ready to have our first child, Wilma was teaching in the public school system of Buffalo, New York. She didn't want the birth of our first child to interrupt her teaching duties during the school year, so she arranged to conceive our first child at a time that would result in a delivery date in the middle of her summer-long vacation. That worked out precisely as planned. Long-range planning helped to determine the birth date of our second child, as well. Wilma knew that my college graduation day would be in the month of May, and she didn't want to be pregnant at that time. So she arranged to conceive at a time that would result in a delivery date two months before my graduation. That, too, went off exactly as planned. In all of my life, I have never heard of any other woman who went to such lengths to determine the birth dates of her children, but that's the way Wilma's mind works, and the whole family has benefitted over the years from that very rare talent of hers. It probably explains why she was able to so effortlessly coordinate all of the children's many activities as well as her many other responsibilities. It was because of women like Wilma that the term "Super Mom" was coined, and no one deserves that title more than she.

Wilma had some amazing parenting skills. To show you how strategic she was in her thinking, I'd like to share with you her technique for potty training the children. She decided very early that she was not going to frustrate herself or the children by trying to potty train them until they were one to two years old and could understand verbal instructions. When she determined that the time was right, she completely potty trained them in just one day. After that day, they never again soiled their diapers in the daytime, and they never again wet the bed at night. This is how she did it. First, she installed a toilet-seat adapter on the toilet to accommodate the child's small size. Then she planned her schedule so that she would be working in the kitchen all morning cooking and cleaning. She brought the child into the kitchen with her and blocked off all exits so the child would have to stay in the kitchen. She removed all of the child's clothing and underwear except for a shirt, and then she gave the child enough water to drink to ensure that he or she would have to urinate within an hour or two. Wilma went about her chores and the child was engrossed in playing with toys that Wilma had brought into the kitchen. Before too long, the child began to urinate. In the past, the child urinated in a diaper and was probably unaware that it was even happening. This time, however, the child saw the stream of urine squirting from his or her body, and the child instinctively stopped it. Wilma immediately took the child to the toilet and gave instructions to let the rest of it out. The children were told to come to the toilet whenever they needed to do that. In that very instant when the children consciously and intentionally stopped the flow of their urine, they gained full control over all of the body's excretory functions and never again soiled themselves day or night. In less than one hour, each child was completely potty trained. We had to clean up one small puddle from the kitchen floor, but we never again had to change any wet diapers or sheets.

The more I reflect on Wilma's performance as a wife and mother, the more I come to realize that her involvement in my life is one more way in which God has chosen to bless me. I have come to realize that I was married to the "virtuous woman" described by King Solomon in Proverbs 31. Solomon says that her value is far greater than that of precious jewels, and that is certainly true of Wilma.

By 1978, Wilma and I had been married for 13 years. Up until then, we had always lived in apartments, and it had never entered my mind that we should buy a house. Wilma, however, felt that it was time for us to have a house of our own. When Wilma thinks that things are not moving fast enough, she begins to nudge them along. She asked a real estate agent to show us some houses that we might consider buying. At that point, the "commitment principle" began to operate. Whenever you commit yourself to do something, forces are set in motion to make it happen.

The very first house that the agent showed us was a nice split-level house with three levels plus a full basement. It had three bedrooms, one full bathroom and two half bathrooms, a living room, dining room, family room, and a den. It had one feature that Wilma really loved and was probably the selling point for her: It had a huge screen-enclosed back porch. Outside behind the house there was a paved patio and a large backyard ringed with tall stately oak trees. The house was out in the suburbs, but it had easy access to the city where we worked. The Lord had led us to an ideal location. The Lord also blessed us to qualify for the house and gave us the means to pay for it. Once again, that pesky little interruption of my life 15 years earlier turned out to be a blessing. The military draft made me eligible for a VA loan with no money down. Once again, God had foreseen my current need and made provision for it years in advance.

Winter Wonderland: A Week at a Ski Resort

One winter, when the children were about ten and eleven years old, we planned a vacation at a ski resort. This was something we had never done before, so I wasn't sure where the idea came from. In hindsight, I think God planted it in our hearts because he knew it was something that we would enjoy. With her usual enthusiasm, Wilma took over the complete planning of the trip. She contacted friends who were experienced skiers and asked them what resort they recommended. Their recommendation was a beautiful, family-friendly resort in far eastern Pennsylvania called Seven Springs.

We loaded up the car and drove through the scenic countryside of western Maryland. There was plenty of snow that winter, but the roads were clear. After about five or six hours of driving, we arrived at one of the most beautiful scenes imaginable. There were beautiful snow-covered mountains all around. Nestled at the base of the mountains was a gorgeous lodge surrounded by various other buildings. It was the kind of scene you normally only see in movies or in pictures of Switzerland. Since it was the Christmas season, the lodge was fully decorated with Christmas trees, wreaths, tinsel, and other colorful decorations. It was truly a winter wonderland. The lodge had every imaginable amenity. There were excellent restaurants, game rooms, a swimming pool, a gym, a bowling alley, and much more. There was plenty to do on and off the slopes.

We got settled in our very comfortable room, had supper, and then gathered around the television to relax and enjoy our first evening at a ski resort. The movie we watched that night was "A Christmas Story." It was about a nerdy, bespectacled little boy who dreamed of getting a BB gun for Christmas. Apparently the boy had been asking his parents for the gun for a long time, and they had always refused, saying, "You'll shoot your eye out." That phrase was repeated over and over throughout the movie, but that didn't stop the boy from dreaming about owning one. During an outdoor recess at school one cold and wintry day, his classmates on the playground talked him into putting his tongue on the freezingly cold flagpole. As soon as he did, his tongue promptly stuck to the frigid flagpole. When the bell rang and recess ended, his classmates went back inside and left him outside still stuck to the flagpole. The movie had many such scenes that had us laughing all evening.

The next morning we had breakfast and then eagerly headed to the equipment building to rent skis and boots. Since we were all beginners, we signed up for lessons. There are three kinds of slopes at this and most other ski resorts: beginner slopes, which are not very steep at all; the intermediate slopes, which are a bit steeper; and the expert slopes, which are for advanced skiers only. After our lessons, we pretty much stayed on the beginner's slopes that first day practicing what we had learned and getting comfortable on our skis. By the next day, all of us except Wilma, I believe, were ready to move on to the intermediate slopes. There are few things in life that are as great as skiing down a mountainside when you know what you're doing and have the skis under control.

There are three basic things that everyone must learn in order to ski safely: how to turn, how to slow down, and how to stop whenever you need to do so. Day after day, we all advanced in our abilities and comfort levels. However, we still stayed on the intermediate slopes. My son, on the other hand, mastered skiing so quickly and thoroughly that he found the intermediate slopes to be too tame for him, and he asked for permission to go on the expert slopes. I was reluctant to let him go, but I didn't want to let my fears hold him back. I told him he could go, but only if I could go with him to make sure I thought he could handle it safely.

From the top of the highest and steepest mountain at the resort, the slope looked daunting. My son fearlessly pushed off, and I followed behind him to make sure he stayed in control and stayed safe. He handled both his speed and his turns with great skill, and much to my surprise, so did I. From that day forward, the entire mountain was ours. Day after day was filled with exhilarating pleasure, and all too quickly the week was over. This vacation will go down in our record books as one of our greatest vacation experiences. We reluctantly returned home, but I had found a new hobby that would provide me with many years of enjoyment. Winter after winter, I traveled all over the northeast exploring many different ski resorts. My only regret is that I didn't get to fulfill my dream of going to the ski resorts in the Rocky Mountain area. Maybe one day.

I believe that God is pleased when his children fully enjoy the life he has given them. Jesus said of his mission here on earth that he had come here so that we might have life and have it more abundantly. Never hesitate to enjoy the wholesome things that God makes available to you.

The Children Find Their Place in the World, and I Enter My Golden Years Still Guided by God's Unseen Hand

When our children were ready for college, we sent them off to my alma mater, Oakwood College. I hoped they would remain there for all four years of college and have the same kind of rich experience I had. I soon realized that what was right for me was not necessarily right for them. God has a different destiny for each person, and each one has to follow his or her own path. God sees the future and knows what experiences we need along the way to prepare us for it. He carefully tailors those experiences for each individual. Both of our children left Oakwood after the first year and went to other colleges in pursuit of their respective goals. Our daughter transferred to Hampton University where she majored in accounting. We were thrilled when she graduated as valedictorian of her class. We were equally thrilled when four major accounting firms offered her a job at their companies. She went to work for a highly prestigious investment company in New York's financial district. That would never have happened if she had followed my path and remained at Oakwood in pursuit of my goal for her. What she accomplished far exceeded anything I had envisioned for her.

Our son also left Oakwood to follow his own path after his first year there. Oakwood did not have the field of study he wanted to pursue, so he transferred to the University of Michigan. A government agency was offering full scholarships to individuals who would major in specific fields and then bring their expertise in that field to the agency for at least five years. Our son won one of those scholarships, and he went into government service upon graduation. God had uniquely crafted a set of experiences that were suited to my son's personality and abilities. It's amazing how God puts you where you need to be and equips you for what lies ahead in your future. After he had fulfilled his five-year obligation to that first agency, he moved to Hollywood and worked in the film and television business. While there, he wrote a movie script and directed and produced an award-winning film based on that script. Years later, he was hired by the Government Printing Office where I used to work. God took us on a totally different journey to a very similar destination. I have seen with my own eyes that God is faithful and that he delivers the blessings that he promises to pour out on those who obey him. These blessings run over onto the children if they live in obedience to his will. With so many blessings awaiting us, why would anyone choose to live any other way? We serve God not for the blessings, but because we love him. If you do not already know him, get a copy of the Bible and read the books of Matthew, Mark, Luke, John, and Acts of the Apostles first or find a Bible-believing church and get to know him for yourself. You will come to love and obey him solely because of who he is. The blessings are just a fringe benefit that comes with that relationship. The blessings must never become your primary goal apart from the relationship.

In 1995, I decided to retire after a long and rewarding career at the Government Printing Office. When I started to work at the printing office, I had no thought in my mind about retirement, and consequently I made no financial preparations for it. However, God looked ahead and put me in a job that provided a comfortable retirement program. God opened just the right doors of opportunity for me at every stage of my life, and he did all of this without my being fully aware of just how thoroughly he was providing for my every need. Without any real forethought or significant effort on my part, God had provided me with cradle-to-grave benefits. That which he has done for me and for others, he will do for you. All you have to do is fully surrender your life to him and let him have his way in your life. Then prepare to be amazed.

I wish I had known in the beginning what I know now about retirement planning. I would have saved and invested more. My advice to young people who are just entering the workforce is that they take the long view of life and not spend everything they earn. Financial advisors say that by saving $100 to $500 a month for 40 years, a person can become a millionaire or a multi-millionaire if the money is properly invested. It takes a bit of discipline, but it is well worth it in the end. To those who are looking for successful financial management strategies, I highly recommend the program taught by Dave Ramsey and the staff at Financial Peace University.

Chapter Four

Observations and Conclusions

After a Retrospective Look at My Life

Finding Something Good in Everything

The Bible says that all things work together for good to those who love God and are called according to his purposes. Initially, it's difficult to see any good in some of the things that happen to us, but if we allow enough time to pass, we will eventually see the accuracy of that biblical promise. At first glance, it seems like a tragedy for a two-year-old child to be separated from his mother and to be placed in an orphanage. However, if I had stayed with my birth mother, I probably would have been raised in the ghetto. That, no doubt, would have shaped my worldview and my image of myself. I probably would have had self-imposed limits on what I could do and what I could become.

As tragic as the separation from my mother was, it turned out to be for my good. If I had not spent time in the orphanage, I would never have met Mr. and Mrs. Williams and been exposed to the wonderful influence they had on me. My years with them gave me the best possible foundation for my life. As terrible as it seemed for me to be uprooted from the Williams household, it was the perfect timing for me to have some great foster brothers with whom I could relate. I benefited so much from that experience, especially in the things I learned about woodworking from Clifford Pinno. It was a real tragedy when Mrs. Mason, our beloved foster mother, lost her battle with cancer, and I had to leave her home. What good could possibly come from that?

If I had not been placed in yet another foster home run by Mrs. Parham, I would not have discovered the book that gave me my spiritual awakening and awareness, nor would I have been where I needed to be to become acquainted with Seventh-day Adventists, an event that shaped the rest of my life.

If any of those tragic and disruptive events had not occurred, I would not have gone to Oakwood College and had all of the wonderful experiences I had there. If I had not gone to Oakwood, I never would have had the terrific career I had at the Government Printing Office, nor would I have met Wilma and had the two wonderful children that I have. I think my life is living proof that all things do indeed work together for good to those who love God and are called according to his purposes. It's a long, slow but steady process all worked out on God's timetable. We can't see beyond the current crisis, but we can know for sure that our future is in God's hands and that he will bring something good out of everything we experience.

What are the odds that any of those events in my life would happen solely by chance? In particular, what are the odds that I would go 1,500 miles away from home to a college that I previously didn't even know existed? What are the odds that while at that obscure little college I would see a tiny little classified ad that would lead to my career and impact the rest of my life? I was not fully cognizant of God's involvement in those events when I was going through them, but a retrospective look at the entirety of my life allows me to see his hand in all of it.

God has a way of putting us where we need to be for our own good and development at any given time. Not everybody needs the same experiences. We are all unique individuals, and our experiences are tailored to our specific needs. God uses every experience we have to prepare us for the next phases of our lives. Enjoy and make the most of each one. Each apparent disruption in my life came at just the right time for me to receive what I needed at that stage of my development.

I don't want to give you the impression that if we fully obey God that life will be a bed of roses and that nothing bad will ever happen. Jesus made it perfectly clear that bad things sometimes happen to good people. He emphasized that point when, in response to a question from his disciples, he said that the man who was born blind had not sinned, nor had his parents. In another instance, he said that those people who were killed when the tower of Siloam fell on them were no worse sinners than anybody else. Sometimes tragedies occur by accident, by poor decisions that we make (we can learn from these), by the actions of bad people, or for reasons that defy explanation. Jesus identified Satan as the source of the bad things that happen on this earth. Jesus told of a woman who had walked around bent over at the waist for 15 years. He said she did that because she had been bound by Satan all of those years. Satan has been causing mischief ever since the beginning of time when he lured Adam and Eve into sin and caused them to lose their garden home and their close relationship with God that they had always enjoyed. The good news is that our relationship with God can be restored through Jesus Christ when we accept him as our Savior. In addition, we also know that when bad things happen, we don't have to face them alone. God is still with us and will help us to get through them. We also have the promise of a brighter day when Jesus will return and put an end to all sin and suffering forever.

In the Bible, Joseph and Job are two examples of very good people to whom some very bad things happened. Joseph's brothers were so jealous of him that they wanted to kill him. Instead, they were persuaded by one of the brothers to sell him to slave traders who took him away to Egypt. While serving in his master's house in Egypt, he was falsely accused of sexual assault against his master's wife, and he was thrown into prison for 13 long years. However, the Bible says that God's favor was upon him during all of his difficulties. Even in prison, the warden gave him an elevated position and put him in charge of the other prisoners. Joseph had the ability to accurately interpret dreams. In God's perfect timing, Joseph was released from prison so he could interpret Pharaoh's dream. Pharaoh was so impressed with Joseph's intelligence that he made him second in command over all of Egypt. Under Joseph's leadership, Egypt and most of the surrounding countries were saved from starvation during a severe famine. None of that would have happened if he had not undergone all of those many years of mistreatment that didn't seem to make any sense at first.

Job was another righteous man who seemed to suffer horribly for no apparent reason. He was a very righteous and devout man who had become quite wealthy and was living a good life. God had showered his blessings on Job and caused whatever he did to prosper. Satan was convinced that Job was only devoted to God because God had so richly blessed him. In order to prove his point, Satan began to take things away from Job one by one in rapid succession. Job owned huge herds of cattle, camels, sheep, and other animals. Satan sent marauders in who took them all away in a single day. He caused a building to collapse and kill Job's children who were inside. Job was smitten with a terrible and debilitating illness that left sores all over his body. His friends and relatives shunned him, and even his wife thought he would be better off dead. Through it all, Job never gave up his faith in God. He famously said, "Even if God slays me, yet will I trust him." When Job's trials were over, God gave him double what he had lost (he got double for his trouble). So be like Job, and trust God no matter what happens. God will help us get through every trial. When bad things happen, we must never give up our trust in God. No matter what happens, God is still in control and, as in these two examples, will often bring something good out of what appears to be something very bad.

–oOo–

Guided by An Unseen Hand

Artist: Robert Hartman. Used by permission of the
Review and Herald Publishing Association.

Christ Rescues Peter During a Storm on the Sea of Galilee

When life gets stormy, his hand will be there for you.

I am absolutely astounded at how often and how wonderfully God has orchestrated events in my life, and I am equally astounded that I didn't recognize it at the time. There were so many things I just took for granted with never so much as a "thank you." Now that I've seen the big picture and uncovered the evidence, I am overflowing with gratitude. I hope that this book will give you an epiphany and bring you to an earlier recognition of God's involvement in your life so you can begin thanking and praising him as you go through life instead of waiting until your golden years to do so.

The best way to detect God's activity in your life is to be in a situation where you are totally dependent on him and your own resources to survive. As long as you are dependent on family, government, or some other entity to provide for your needs, you are less likely to look to God or to see his participation in your life. I believe we are all expected to go on what I call an "Abrahamic journey." As the father of the nation of Israel, Abraham was a very prominent person in the Bible. He was a very prosperous man who had huge and diverse herds of livestock and no doubt had sizeable quantities of the traditional symbols of wealth such as gold, silver, and fine jewels. He lived in the same city as his father, uncles, aunts, cousins, nieces, and nephews. He no doubt felt quite comfortable and secure in Ur of the Chaldees, which was the name of the city where he lived. He probably never thought of leaving Ur. Then, one day God directed him to pack up and leave Ur and go to a distant place that God would later show him. God gave him no details about his destination. Abraham's trust in God was so strong and complete that he started out on his journey even though he didn't know where he was going or what he would find when he got there.

All of us are required to go on a journey similar to Abraham's. Not all of us are called upon to leave our hometown or go far away from our roots. However, all of us have to find our own way in life, depending solely on God plus the skills and resources he has given us. Like Abraham, we must be willing to follow that journey wherever it leads. Just because we don't immediately know our ultimate destination doesn't mean we are wandering aimlessly. God knows the destination and the timetable, and at just the right time, he will bring us to our destination.

This principle of "taking the journey" manifests itself throughout all of nature. Upon reaching maturity, the vast majority of animals leave their birth family, start a new family, and find their own way in the world. Sometimes, young wolves are reluctant to leave the wolf pack into which they were born, and they are repeatedly chased away by their mothers. For a while, the reluctant young wolves keep coming back. Over and over again, the very determined mother runs aggressively toward her mature young wolves, growling at them until they get the message that they are to find their own path and place in life. Young birds that refuse to leave the nest are pushed out by their mothers. If all goes well, the young bird will instinctively flap its wings while falling. That may be the moment when the young fledgling first realizes that it, too, can fly just like its parents. Then it will fly away to begin life on its own. God forms a one-on-one relationship with every single one of his creatures, including humans. That's why the Bible says that not a single sparrow falls to the ground without his notice. How privileged we are that our maker wants to be that intimately involved in our lives.

Six Life Principles

God wants to help us realize our greatest potential and reach our highest level of fulfillment. In order for that to happen, there are several things that we must do:

1. Just like Abraham, we must be willing to go to places where we've never been before and do things we've never done. Adaptability is critically important. If we are unwilling to leave our current comfort zone, it severely limits what God is able to do to improve our lot in life. Since God watches over the sparrows, it is certain that he watches over us. Wherever we go and whatever we do, we can be sure that God is with us and is working on our behalf to produce the best possible outcome for us.

    All too often, we get comfortably situated in a certain environment, and we are reluctant to leave it. This is what is known as our "comfort zone." In that zone, we have familiar friends, relatives, places we go, and work to do. It is understandable that we would be reluctant to leave our comfort zone, but often our best future can be found in another place. Unless we are adaptable enough to make a move, we can often limit what God is able to do for us. Adaptability and faith in God are essential elements in our growth and advancement. We can go anywhere with the knowledge that wherever we go, God goes with us and will quickly turn our new environment into another place of comfort for us. He does it for the sparrow, and he'll do it for you.

2. We must live our lives free from irrational and unjustified fear.

    The Bible says that God does not give us a spirit of fear, so any fears that we have come from our own imaginations or from the whisperings of Satan, who is the enemy of our souls. King Solomon had a very colorful way of expressing himself. In Proverbs 26:13, he says that the lazy man imagines that there are lions roaming the streets. Consequently, he will not go outside. He fills his mind with all sorts of imaginary fears that prevent him from doing anything. Like the man in Solomon's proverb, most of our fears spring forth from our imaginations. They are completely without foundation and have no basis in reality. They keep us from experiencing life fully and from enjoying it as God intended. Knowing these facts, we should be resolved that we will immediately dismiss any unjustified fears from our minds and give them no place in our thinking. Fear can paralyze a person and prevent one from fulfilling God's purposes and plans for their lives. I have a friend who had a superb singing voice when he was a teenager. His talent was so great that organizations all over town invited him to sing for their groups. He always got thunderous applause and rave reviews. He caught the attention of wealthy patrons who had so much confidence in his abilities that they offered to pay for him to go to school at Julliard School of Music. Then something awful happened. He developed an overwhelming case of stage fright, and he turned down the scholarship offer. His singing ability was obviously a gift from God that was intended to be his destiny and would have led him on to fame and fortune. He allowed fear to thwart God's purposes for his life. Fear destroys more dreams and dashes more hopes than almost anything else. Don't let it rob you of your dreams or frustrate God's plans for your life.

Over and over again, the Bible admonishes us to banish fear from our lives. In order for us to get the message, the Bible uses such words as "fear not," "be not afraid," "let not your heart be troubled, neither let it be afraid," and "don't be anxious about anything." We would do well to heed those instructions. It will give you great peace of mind and self-confidence as you go about your daily life. Don't allow fear to thwart God's plans for your life and rob you of your destiny.

The admonition to avoid fear is a constant theme throughout the Bible because God knows how devastating it can be. It is one of the principal weapons in Satan's arsenal. Don't allow him to use it on you.

One way to avoid fear is to "live in the moment." Jesus was trying to teach his disciples that lesson when he told them not to be anxious about tomorrow. It is essential to plan for tomorrow, but that's different from worrying about it. He said that we have quite enough to be concerned about today without being anxious about tomorrow. It's alright to reflect on the past or to plan for the future as long as neither one of those activities is a cause for anxiety. Even God's name implies that we should live in the moment. Moses was a righteous and godly man who had such a close relationship with God that he could speak with God face to face. On one occasion, Moses asked God what his name was, and God replied by saying that his name is "I Am." That may seem like an odd name for the creator of the universe to give himself, but there is much profound meaning in that name. By telling us that his name is "I Am," he is essentially saying that he is ever-present and we need not worry about previous mistakes we have made or about painful experiences from our past. He's also saying that we need not worry about the future because he'll be there with us when it arrives. He is with us moment by moment in the present, and that's all we need to know in order to have complete peace of mind. So stay in the moment. That's where God is, and he's the source of everything you need. That's why his name is "I Am." Read Matthew 6:28 and Luke 12:27 for more of what Jesus has to say about living in the moment.

The apostle Paul said that he had learned to be content under all circumstances. That is a wonderful state of mind to have because it means that you are completely relying on God and trusting him to supply all of your needs. With that level of contentment comes a kind of peace that passes all understanding. It keeps us free from all anxiety, and fear can find no place in a mind that is so contented.

Freedom from fear comes when we have complete faith and trust in God. The Bible says that the person who keeps his mind on God will be kept in perfect peace. It also says, "Great peace have they that love your law, and nothing shall offend them." Avail yourself of that peace, and banish fear from your life.

If you do feel fear, take comfort in the knowledge that you are not alone. Some of the bravest among us have felt fear at one time or another. The psalmist, David, was a man of unquestioned bravery. He fought a lion, a bear, a giant, and numerous invading armies, and he came away victorious every time, but there were times when even he was afraid. He handled those fears by saying, "Whenever I am afraid, I will trust in [God]" (Psalm 56:3). When fear creeps into your consciousness, don't allow it to take up residence there. Do as David did, and dismiss it by putting your trust in God. It is surprising how quickly fear disappears when you do that.

3. Dare to dream big dreams, and then go to work to fulfill them. If you watch for it, you will see God's involvement in every aspect of your project.

Many people become so accustomed to their current circumstances that it never occurs to them that those circumstances can be changed. With God's help, you can change your circumstances if you really want to and if you dare to believe that you can. Just because you've lived all of your life in the ghetto doesn't mean you have to stay there. Picture yourself living where you would like to live, and then go to work and plan toward it. You'll be amazed at what God will do to help you fulfill your dream. If you don't like the job or limited education you have, dare to dream of something more, and then work toward achieving it. Do not allow yourself to be limited by your past or current circumstances. We are often limited by the size of our dreams.

The importance of having a dream cannot be overemphasized. Dreams intensify and increase God's involvement in our lives. God loves and sustains us all, but he does not need to become very involved in the life of someone who sits around and does nothing all day, but he does have to frequently come to the aid of the dreamer and the doer. That's why Solomon said that "where there is no vision [or dream], the people perish." We literally start to shrivel from reduced interaction with God. Benjamin Franklin put it this way: "God helps those who help themselves." That's not just a cleverly worded cliché. There is great profundity and truth in that statement.

Your dream may be as small as completing a crossword puzzle or reading a good book, but try always to have a goal toward which you are striving. Don't let there be long periods of time when your brain is idle and unstimulated by a challenge of some sort. The brain that is active stimulates the creation of new neural connections. Just as muscles atrophy from not being used, so can the mind.

I don't believe there is such a point in one's life, but if you are at that stage in life where big dreams are not practical, then dream small dreams, but never stop dreaming. Your very life and connectivity with God depend on it.

4. Learn to utilize the power of commitment. There is nothing more powerful than a person whose mind is made up. The fulfillment of any dream does not come by wishful thinking. It comes when we commit ourselves to that dream and take action to make it happen. The two key words are "commitment" and "action." The fusion of those two words brings results.

Commitment and action are expressions of faith, and God always responds to faith by bringing to our attention the knowledge, resources, and people who we need to help us achieve our goals. As I look back over the events of my life, a clear and consistent pattern emerges. When I do what I can do to achieve a goal, God gets involved and does what I cannot do. From the moment I commit to a goal and take action to achieve it, everything seems to fall in place. This pattern repeats itself so consistently that it appears to be a universal principle upon which we can depend. The opposite principle also seems to be true: If we make no commitments and take no action, nothing will ever change. God truly does help those who help themselves.

5. Look both near and far for opportunities to improve your life or create your own opportunities. At just the right time, God will open doors of opportunity for you. When he does, go through every one of them immediately and without hesitation. The doors of opportunity only stay open for a limited time. It's a sad reality that God frequently opens doors of opportunity for people and they refuse to go through them because of fear or a reluctance to leave one's comfort zone, and the opportunity slips away. Don't let that be the case with you.

Many people never seek new opportunities simply because it never occurs to them to do so. Others fail to seek new opportunities because they are reluctant to try anything new or unfamiliar. When we realize that God is directing our lives, we need not have any such reluctance. When God opens a door of opportunity, he often leads us into totally new and unfamiliar situations, but he never leads us into anything that is beyond our capabilities. He will always enable us to rise to the occasion. Sometimes he leads us into new situations to increase our capabilities. Sometimes he does so to help us discover capabilities we didn't know we had. Whenever God opens a door of opportunity, go through it with the assurance that he is with you wherever you go and will help you succeed.

6. In addition to the Ten Commandments, there are numerous other commandments in the Bible (e.g.: "Love your neighbor as you love yourself," "Do unto others as you would have them do unto you," "Give, and it shall be given unto you," etc.). The best way to detect God's involvement in your everyday life is to make a commitment to obey all of God's commandments. The reason I say that is because many of God's commandments have some very specific promises associated with them, and fulfillment of those promises is conditioned upon our obedience to the commandments. When you start to obey those commandments, God goes to work to fulfill his promises. He will do it in ways that will absolutely amaze you. When you see that happening over and over again in a wide variety of ways, there will be no doubt in your mind that it is he who is at work fulfilling his promises.

How to Maintain the Flow of God's Blessings Into Your Life

Is it possible to interrupt the flow of God's blessings? Absolutely! You may ask what it might be that could cause such an interruption. To put it briefly, the one-word answer is "sin." When we deviate from what God wants us to do or not do, we cause damage to the pipeline, and we can expect an interruption in the flow of God's blessings. The third chapter of 1 Peter says, "For the eyes of the Lord are over the righteous, and his ears are open to their prayers, but the face of the Lord is against them that do evil." So sin alters one's relationship with God, and can interrupt the flow of his blessings into one's life.

The Bible contains numerous examples that show how sin interrupts the flow of God's blessings. In no uncertain terms, it makes clear just what the devastating effects of sin are. Isaiah 59:2 says, "Your iniquities [sins] have caused a separation between you and your God." That verse alone should be enough to make every person flee from sin, but there are even more reasons to avoid it. Jeremiah 5:25 says, "Your sins have caused good things to be withheld from you." Those verses show that there is a direct correlation between your behavior and the amount of blessings you receive or fail to receive. The Bible also says in Jeremiah 16 that when Israel sinned, God took away his peace, lovingkindness, and mercies from them. He also took away their joy and gladness. In reality, Israel forfeited those things by their own bad behavior. God takes sin very seriously, and so should we.

The Bible also says that "... the way of the transgressor is hard." David learned those lessons the hard way: David had been blessed and favored in everything he did. He had everything, including wealth, power, and prestige. Then he deviated from God's will by committing adultery with another man's wife and impregnating her. He compounded his sin by sending the husband into a fierce battle where he was sure to be killed. David's life was never the same after that. He encountered one problem after another, including a temporarily successful attempt by his own son to overthrow him and seize the kingdom. David had to leave the palace and flee into the wilderness with a small number of loyal followers. He was on the run for a while until the rebellion could be put down. When David sinned, God removed the hedge of protection that had been around him all of his life. This gave the enemy of our souls access to David that had previously been denied, and now Satan was free to cause all sorts of problems for David. In Romans 6, the Bible says that we are the servants of the one whom we choose to obey. In this world, there are only two choices: God or Satan. If we do that which is right, we become the servants of God, and our lives will be blessed. However, if we choose to sin, we become the servants of Satan, and terrible consequences come from making that choice. We never want to forgo God's blessings and protection by choosing to sin. The way of the transgressor is indeed very hard.

For other examples of how sin interrupts the flow of God's blessings, read in the Bible about Adam and Eve, Samson, King Solomon, King Saul, Ahab, and many others. There is hope, however, for those who sin and interrupt the flow of God's blessings into their lives. In Luke 15, Jesus told a parable about a prodigal son who wanted to get out from under his father's strict rules and start living life his own way. So impatient was he to get away that he couldn't wait until his father's demise to get his inheritance. He demanded it immediately, and the father gave it to him. The son left home immediately and, in a very short time, he had spent his entire inheritance on all kinds of sin and debauchery. He found himself to be hungry, destitute, and without hope. When he hit bottom, he repented of his sins and returned to his father to beg his forgiveness. He knew he didn't deserve to have the privileges of being a son, so he begged to be hired as a servant in his father's house. Instead of scolding him or rejecting him for his shameful behavior, the father eagerly welcomed him back and restored their relationship. The father so completely forgave the errant son that it was as if he had never sinned. The parable of the prodigal son presents a classic example of what happens when we make the wrong choice. It also presents a classic example of what happens when we repent of our sins and return to God. He always welcomes us back into his favor as he did when David repented, confessed his sins, and turned back to him.

Another thing that will interrupt the flow of God's blessings into your life is pride. I'm not talking about the kind of pride that causes a person to be pleased with his or her accomplishments. The kind of pride to which I am referring is characterized by boastfulness and arrogance. When God pours out his blessings upon you, and you start to take credit for them, or boast about them, or start to think that you are better than other people, you are guilty of the sin of pride or arrogance. God is very displeased with that kind of behavior and attitude. Take a moment to read the entirety of Deuteronomy, chapter 8. It will humble you. You will realize that when you succeed and prosper in life, it is not solely due to your own efforts. You are actually witnessing God's direct involvement in your everyday life. Few things will interrupt the flow of God's blessings faster than pride. I'm beginning to think that pride is at or near the top of the list of things that displease God. Take a look at what God has to say about pride:

1. God resists the proud and gives grace to the humble
   (1 Peter 5:5 and James 4:6).

2. Whosoever exalts himself shall be abased [or brought down low], and he that humbles himself shall be exalted [lifted up or elevated] (Matthew 23:12).

3. Pride goes before destruction, and a haughty spirit before a fall
   (Proverbs 16:18).

In a famous parable, Christ illustrates the differences between pride and humility. He shows what God's attitude is toward those who are proud and boastful. In the parable, two men went into the temple to pray side by side. One was a wealthy man who boasted in his prayer about all of the good things he had done and how he was better than other people. By contrast, the poor man praying beside him was so humble and contrite that he bowed before God and would not even lift up his eyes toward heaven. He confessed that he was an unworthy sinner, and he asked for God's mercy. Christ essentially said that God deemed the poor man's prayer to be more acceptable. In that parable, it's interesting to note what Christ said about the rich man's prayer. He said, "He prayed thus with himself." He wasn't praying to God. He was praying to others who might overhear his long list of accomplishments. One can reasonably conclude that God is extremely displeased with such prayers and attitudes. If you want to keep God's blessings flowing into your life, avoid pride like the plague. God really does hate it because it's totally unjustified. After all, as the apostle Paul says, "What do you have that you were not given [by God]?" (1 Corinthians 4:7).

Sadly, I can provide a personal example of how God's blessings can be interrupted when we deviate from God's will. Several years ago, my wife and I were having problems in our marriage that we considered to be irreconcilable, and we decided to get a divorce.

As with the characters in the Bible who sinned, God did not completely abandon us, but there were major disruptions in the previously endless flow of his blessings into our lives. Our problems began almost immediately. Wilma decided to go work with a group of missionaries in Argentina. The group was constructing buildings in a poor region of the country, and Wilma was assigned the job of smoothing the outside walls of the building using sandpaper. For some of the sanding work, she had to reach areas above her head. Inevitably, she breathed in a considerable amount of dust and developed what we hope are only some short-term respiratory problems. If she had been with me where she should have been, one of two things would have happened that would have prevented that problem: (1) she would not have gone to Argentina, or (2) I would have gone with her and would have made sure she protected both her eyes and her nose from the dust with goggles and a cloth over her nose.

My and Wilma's misfortunes since our divorce show that when you're not where you're supposed to be and not doing what you're supposed to be doing, unpleasant things sometimes happen that would not ordinarily happen.

I was retired by then, and I drifted around the country like a vagabond trying to decide where to settle down. I spent a few years in one city after another before settling in Florida. During those years, one tragedy after another befell me. I'll mention just a few of them (there are plenty more). I was riding on a city bus that was involved in an accident, and I ended up with a broken arm. The doctor who treated me took so many X-rays that the nerves in that arm and hand were damaged. In the course of my treatment, I had to go to numerous medical facilities, each one of which required my social security number. Somewhere along the way, my identity was stolen and misused, possibly in a way that could adversely affect my credit. In one place where I was staying, there was a defective microwave oven that was leaking radiation, and I was exposed to it. In another incident, I was standing at a bus stop when a teenager asked me if I had change for a twenty-dollar bill. When I took out the money, he snatched it from my hand and left without giving me the twenty-dollar bill he had pretended to have.

None of those kinds of things had ever happened to me before in my entire life. I had always been favored and protected until I chose to deviate from God's will for my life. One day I was telling my daughter about my misfortunes. She wisely and accurately said that all of those terrible things were happening because I wasn't where I was supposed to be. She was absolutely right. If I had been with my wife, I would not have been in any of these places where those things happened.

I would like to share with you one of the most important lessons I learned from this experience: Never make a decision of that magnitude without first considering what God has to say about it. Belatedly, I did decide to see what he has to say about divorce. It turns out that he has quite a lot to say about it, and it should come as no surprise that he is very strongly opposed to it. I would like to discuss several of the things the Bible has to say about divorce:

1. In one place, God says it is better not to make a vow than to make one and not keep it. In Malachi 2:16, God says that he hates divorce. That fact alone should deter everyone from even considering divorce except in the most extreme and dangerous cases. Why would anyone deliberately do something knowing that God hates it and is adamantly opposed to it? That's tantamount to saying that we know better than God what's best for us, or even worse, that we don't care what God thinks. That's the height of arrogance and rebellion. That's a self-destructive position for anybody to take, especially a Christian who should know better.

2. In Matthew 19:6, Jesus said, "What God has joined together, let no man put asunder." The words "no man" includes the two people in the marriage. Jesus is essentially saying that marriage is God's handiwork. It's not something trivial that we do on a whim and discard just as easily. It is never advisable to tamper with God's handiwork.

3. In Matthew 6:15, Jesus also said that if we do not forgive others, God will not forgive us. Don't take lightly the words of Jesus when he says that we will not be forgiven if we don't forgive others. Don't think that he doesn't really mean that. There is no greater authority than Jesus on what God will or will not do. I would take him at his word. Usually, when a couple is considering divorce, one or both parties are unwilling to forgive the other. It is extremely unwise to put yourself in a position where God cannot forgive you. It's frightening just to contemplate it. Just imagine yourself missing out on the chance to go to heaven simply because you couldn't forgive someone. The only way to get into heaven is to have all of your sins forgiven. If you have put yourself in a position where God cannot forgive you, then you have shut yourself out of heaven. Unforgiveness should be avoided at all costs. Your eternal destiny depends on it.

4. God commands husbands to love their wives, and he commands wives to respect their husbands and to submit to them. If a marriage is in trouble, the parties in the marriage have to ask themselves if they have intentionally and consistently done everything God has commanded them to do in that regard. Husbands, have you shown love toward your wife consistently as God has commanded you? Wives, are you giving your husband the kind of respect the Bible requires you to give? The Bible also says that wives were specifically created for the purpose of being a helpmeet for their husbands. Wives, are you facilitating your husband's activities in every way you can? If

Observations and Conclusions After a Retrospective Look at My Life

you are contemplating a divorce, the chances are that you haven't been doing all that God requires of you. Before you take that fateful step, try doing what God commands you to do, and see if your attitudes toward each other don't change and if divorce can be averted. You absolutely can't go wrong when you do things God's way. A lot of women recoil at the thought of submitting to their husbands, but those who have done it say that it brings out the best in their husbands and did not diminish them in the slightest. I have heard a number of testimonies by people who have saved or dramatically improved their marriages by simply obeying just those two commandments. God's ways really work. It stands to reason that our maker would know what's best for us. You can never go wrong by doing what God says.

Over the years, I've heard numerous testimonials by couples whose marriages were in trouble and on the verge of divorce. One person in the relationship decided to change his or her attitude and do everything God had commanded them to do concerning basic Christian principles of living (love, patience, forgiveness, etc.) and everything God had commanded them concerning their role in the marriage relationship. Usually within a matter of weeks or months, the other spouse noticed the change in the atmosphere of the home and responded in kind. Many marriages have been saved and divorce has been avoided when only one spouse decides to do things God's way. Be brave enough to take the first step toward reconciliation, even if you initially have to do it alone.

When it comes to marriage and divorce or how we will live our lives in general, there are only two choices: We can do things our way or God's way. Those who are wise will do things God's way every time. If the above-mentioned facts had been brought to my attention beforehand, I never would have made the decision to get a divorce. If you are contemplating a divorce, I hope that this information will keep you from making the same mistake I made. Make the right choice so God's blessings can continue to flow into your life without interruption.

If sharing my experience will keep just one person from getting a divorce, then at least something good will have come from it.

That concludes the story of my life and some of the lessons I learned from observing God's involvement in my everyday life. I hope it will cause you to take a closer look at events in your life and that you will more readily see and recognize God's involvement in your own life.

So far, I have related numerous experiences that show God's direct involvement in my life. Now, I would like to present some examples from other people's lives to demonstrate that my experiences are not unique to me. God is actively involved in everyone's life, especially the lives of those who earnestly seek to know and obey him. My first such story is about a good friend of mine named Al. When Al was a teenager about to finish high school, he was very industrious. During that time, he worked at four different jobs to provide himself some income. One of those jobs included operating a clothing press in a laundry and dry cleaning company. After graduating from high school, he decided to take the Air Force entrance exam. He scored so high on the exam that the Air Force pursued him relentlessly in an effort to get him to enlist. Around that time, an Adventist evangelist named Eric Ward was conducting evangelistic meetings in Al's neighborhood. Al was not interested in the meetings, but his father was. His father went alone and enjoyed it so much that he began to urge Al to go with him. At first, Al declined his invitations. After all, that was in the 1950s when television was something new, and Al was more interested in staying home and watching his favorite TV programs.

Al's father persisted in inviting him to the meetings. Finally, in an effort to get his father off of his back, Al consented to go to one meeting. Al was so intrigued by the evangelist's message that he started going to the meetings every night, and he ended up joining the Adventist Church even before his father did. Thus began Al's lifelong walk with God.

Al had to make a big decision regarding his future career. He desperately wanted to join the Air Force, and the Air Force was just as eager to have him, but he knew that if he enlisted, he might not be able to get the Sabbath off from duty. Recruiters assured him that it could be worked out, but Al was skeptical. The lure of an Air Force career was so strong that Al actually went down to the recruitment office to enlist. Would he put God first or his career ambitions? With his hand on the doorknob of the recruitment office, he decided to put God first. He turned around and went back home, still uncertain about what he would do for a career.

With the most impeccable timing, God intervened. At about that time, an Adventist minister from Al's region was about to make a trip to Oakwood College, and he invited Al to go along. Having nothing else to do, Al agreed to go. When he got to the campus, he fell in love with it and decided that he wanted to go to school there. The only problem was that he didn't have the money for it. His family had set aside money for a college fund, but there was only enough money in it to send one person to college, and he had unselfishly decided that the money should be used to send his sister to nursing school. What was he to do?

Al learned about the work-study program at Oakwood and decided that it was how he would finance his education. To his delight, he discovered that God's unseen hand had already been at work preparing the way for him. Business at the college laundry had increased so much that they had a desperate need for workers who knew how to operate the pressing machines in the laundry. Just a short while earlier, God had foreseen this opportunity and prepared him for it.

While Al was pursuing his education in biological sciences, the Army sent him a draft notice, but God intervened, enabling him to get a student deferment that kept him out of the service until he could complete his education. For me, God had used the military service to advance his plans for my life, and for Al, he used a deferment to advance his purposes. Al later went into the service, but the timing was perfect for him. Al went on to have a distinguished career in his field, and he is now retired. His life is another example of how well things work out when we let go of the reins and let God have control of our lives. As King Solomon said in the book of Proverbs, "Trust in the Lord with all of your heart, and lean not upon your own understanding. In all of your ways, acknowledge him, and he shall direct your paths." God does it so much better than we ever could. Al's story is an example of how richly God rewards those who are faithful and obedient to him.

Another example of God's unseen hand at work is the story of a good friend of mine named Candida. She is a widow in her mid-eighties and has been a devout Christian for most of her life. When I met her, she was retired, had her own home in a senior community, and was living quite comfortably. Her only concern was the fact that her daughter lived and worked two hours to the east of her and her granddaughter and great-grandchildren lived two hours to the north of her, and she longed for more frequent contact with them. She was also concerned about what would happen if there was a medical emergency and no one discovered it in time (those medical alert buttons don't cover every kind of emergency).

Candida had raised her granddaughter, and they were very close. For years, the granddaughter had urged Candida to move in with her family of five. Candida very much appreciated the offer and the thoughtfulness that had prompted it, but she declined each offer. She felt that the house would be too crowded. Besides, she was a very independent person who was well able to take care of herself. She also valued having private time occasionally. Candida knows the power of prayer, and so she prayed earnestly about the matter.

Candida's very devoted granddaughter was determined to find a way to get them closer together so the entire family could have daily physical contact. That's when God stepped in and provided what can only be described as a miracle. He brought to the granddaughter's attention a foreclosed house that was available in a senior community located just seven minutes away from the granddaughter's house. The best part of the story is that the bank only wanted $3,500 to get the property off its books. Candida moved quickly and bought the house immediately. It is a much bigger and better house located in a nicer community than where she had been living at the time. In addition to all of those wonderful blessings, she was able to rent out her former residence, and it now provides her with extra income. Her family went to work and had her moved into her new house in less than a week. She is much happier now and gets to see her family every day. You could call that a very lucky set of events, but you would be completely missing the overwhelming evidence of

Guided by An Unseen Hand

God's involvement in the matter. Candida's experience provides ample evidence of God's involvement in our everyday lives and of his willingness to answer our prayers in ways that amaze us. Just as God's unseen hand has been at work in these lives and mine, so will it be in yours. Look for it, and follow his lead.

From the history of America comes yet another unmistakable example of God's involvement in the lives of people. During the Revolutionary War, the continental army was in danger of losing the war. At one point, a contingent of George Washington's army was trapped at a certain location, and a large fleet of British soldiers was sailing down the river toward the Americans. Vastly superior in numbers and firepower, the British soldiers would have easily defeated Washington's ragtag band of soldiers. If that had happened, the revolution would have been over, and America would have ceased to exist as an independent nation.

George Washington desperately needed a miracle, and he got one. As the British flotilla was closing in on his location, a very dense fog settled over the region. In addition, an extremely strong wind blew the British flotilla backward quite a long distance. Under the cover of the fog, Washington's troops were able to escape across the river and avoid what would have been a certain defeat. When the last of Washington's troops got across the river, the fog lifted and the wind ceased to blow. Without God's involvement in that way, there would have been no American nation as we know it today. God not only involves himself in the lives of individuals, but also in the affairs of nations. The Lord's blessings rest upon those nations that have him as their God. George Washington himself said that there is no way that America could have survived without God's help. This and other events from America's history confirm his assertion.

There are numerous Bible verses that reveal just how closely God is involved in our lives, but one of my favorites is Psalm 139, which says:

"You have searched me and known me. You know when I sit down and when I get up. You understand my thoughts even at a distance. You surround my path and my lying down and are familiar with my ways. There is not a word in my mouth that you do not know about. You are in front of me and behind me. Such knowledge is too much for me to comprehend. Where shall I go to escape from you or to get away from you? If I ascend up into heaven, you are there. If I make my bed in the grave, you are there also. If I take the wings of the morning, and dwell in the most remote parts of the sea, even there shall your hand lead me, and your right hand shall hold me. If I think that night will hide me, even the darkness shall be light around me. The darkness doesn't hide anything from you. Instead, the night shines as brightly as the day. The darkness and the light are alike to you … When I awake, I am still with you …"

The apostle Paul expressed the same thought when he said, "In [God] we live and move and have our being" (Acts 17:28). In Jeremiah 23, God makes the following statement about himself: "Am I a god at hand says the Lord, and not a god afar off? Can anyone hide himself in secret places that I shall not see him says the Lord. Do not I fill heaven and earth says the Lord?"

The clear message of those Bible verses is that God is everywhere all of the time. It is true that God is everywhere, but he's not just a hovering presence that passively watches everything we do. Like any good parent, he is actively involved in helping us to fulfill our dreams and our destiny.

Some of my favorite Bible verses are as follows: "Draw near to God, and he will draw near to you" (James 4:8); ". . . You shall seek me and find me when you search for me with all your heart" (Jeremiah 29:13); and "If you seek him, he will be found by you" (1 Chronicles 28:9). Those promises give us the assurance that if we approach God earnestly, we will see the evidence of his involvement in our lives. There is nothing that will give us greater peace of mind and confidence than the knowledge that God is always with us and always available. We do not have to find our way through life alone. We are guided by an unseen hand. Look for that unseen hand in your life, and cooperate with it fully. Follow it wherever it leads you, and it will take you to heights and places you never dreamed were possible. I am going to end this book by quoting the same Bible verse that I used at the beginning. I hope you will make it your motto. "Trust in the Lord with all of your heart, and lean not to your own understanding. In all of your ways, acknowledge him, and he shall direct your paths." God loves us all so much that he gives direction to everyone's life to the extent that we will allow him to do so. The Bible says that he causes his rain to fall on the just and the unjust (Matthew 5:45). However, he will not override our free will and our freedom to choose our own path in life. The amount of his involvement in our lives is limited only by the choices we make. If you choose to willingly and completely submit your life to him in obedience to his word, your life will be guided all the way to the end by his unseen hand.

Note: Please read the remaining few pages of this book, including the Tribute and the Endnotes. Those pages provide even more wonderful examples of God's involvement in our everyday lives. They also provide some amazing facts that you will want to know about several important Bible doctrines.

Artist: Robert Ayres. Used by permission of the
Review and Herald Publishing Association.

The Second Coming of Jesus Christ

One day soon, the invisible hand will be made visible.

A Tribute

to

My Many Mothers

Everybody has at least one mother. I was blessed to have ten wonderful mothers who were willing instruments through whom God could show his love for me. I would like to pay a special tribute to them for their sacrifice and for all that they contributed to my life and to my wellbeing.

1. Let me take this opportunity to say how grateful I am that my birth mother did not abort me as so many unwed mothers do today. If she had, I would not have been here to enjoy all of the many things and blessings that God had planned for me. God has a plan and a purpose for every child conceived, and it's so sad that millions of them never get to experience it. Life is God's gift, and no life should be taken by abortion. With God, the circumstances surrounding one's birth are not important. What is important is what a person does with his or her life. I want to thank my birth mother for letting me have my chance at life.

    I would also like to thank my birth mother for her decision to give up custody of me, not just once, but multiple times. The first time was when I was two years old and she became too ill to properly care for me. After she was well again, she could have regained custody of me at any time, but I think she knew I was better off in the foster homes where I was living than I would have been with her. Regaining custody of me may have been on her mind when I was twelve years old and she visited me at Mrs. Parham's house. I think she sensed that I was happy where I was and decided not to disrupt my life. My entire future would have been completely different if she had taken me back at that point, and the happiness I have enjoyed is due in large part to her decision to leave things as they were. I know how difficult it must have been to make that decision. Thanks, Mom, for loving me enough to let me go.

2. Mrs. Louise Williams had raised three of her four children to adulthood, and she could have relaxed and looked forward to grandchildren. Instead, her great love of children and her compassion for orphans led her to take me into her home. She and her family provided such a warm and nurturing environment that I could not have asked for anything better. Most importantly, she introduced me to God, both at home and at church. Thank you, Mrs. Williams, for giving me such a strong foundation on which to build the rest of my life.

3. Mrs. Mason was one of the most serene and even-tempered people I have ever known, and her demeanor set the tone for the whole house. She calmly performed her duties, working hard practically all day, every day, cooking, cleaning, and providing for her large household that consisted of her husband, four foster boys, and her three adult relatives. By example and by assignment of mandatory duties, she instilled in us a strong work ethic, which helped me to excel in every job I have had and even in my personal life. God brought her into my life at just the right stage of my development to prepare me for the future. I actually believe that bringing different mothers into my life at different stages of my development was better for me than the stability of having one mother throughout my childhood. God picked the right one at just the right time. I will forever be grateful for Mama Mason's love, discipline, and steadiness during that time.

4. By the time I moved into Mattie Parham's house, I had become a voracious reader. Not only did she have a small collection of books, but she had a desk that wasn't being used. I immediately claimed it as mine. The desk was located in front of a window, so there was good lighting. I spent hours there doing my homework and reading whatever I could get my hands on. It was in Mrs. Parham's collection of books that I discovered the book that triggered a profound spiritual awakening in me. Previously I had known about God, but now I wanted to know him and serve him. That book made me more keenly aware of God's presence and involvement in my life than any other book I had read. It led me to begin a lifelong practice of continually reading the entire Bible over and over again. I needed to be in Mrs. Parham's home for that to happen, and God arranged it at just the right point in my life. I want to thank Mrs. Parham for providing the right environment where that could happen.

5. When I was 16, I needed a place where I could freely practice my newfound faith. Once again, God made it happen with no effort on my part. At the request of my pastor, Mrs. Patterson opened her home and took me in, and I flourished under her care. She and her husband made me feel so very welcomed in their home, and it was there that I became both physically and

spiritually mature. I want to thank Mrs. Patterson for providing a safe haven where I could mature enough to go off to college and begin life on my own. Her home was just what I needed at that point in my life. Only God could have arranged it so well.

6. All of my foster parents up to this point in my life had received financial assistance for my care because I was still a minor under the care of the city government. When I arrived at the door of Hortense Davis, I was 20 years old, and no financial assistance was available. Of all my many mothers, she had the fewest of this world's goods to give, but in a certain way, she gave more than all of the others. Although she and I started out with a landlady-and-tenant arrangement, she quickly changed all of that and drew me into her family as her son. I was soon eating with her family and living rent-free at her insistence. If I needed anything or merely wanted something, she would find a way to get it for me—even if she had to borrow money from a neighbor to do it. Even to this day, some 56 years later, I am still astounded at how much pure and unselfish love flowed through her heart. She holds a place of special honor in my pantheon of many mothers.

7. I call Luberta George the "merry widow." She had a lively, almost mischievous sense of humor, and her laughter was so infectious that I found myself laughing a lot. She was an absolute delight to be with. For only a token amount of rent, she provided me with my own private room and access to the whole house. She, like all of my previous mothers, accepted me without hesitation or reservation, and I was immediately treated as if I had been in the family forever. I am still amazed at how God managed to find the perfect place for me time after time.

8. Over the years, Esther Logan has taken numerous college students and former students into her home. The one thing that can be said of her is that she truly loved every one of them. You could see it on her face whenever one of us walked into the house. Her whole face would light up, her eyes would sparkle, and each one of us was welcomed every time with a broad smile and a warm greeting. No mother ever welcomed her own child with greater enthusiasm. Most of the students stayed there only a few months or a couple of years at the most. I, however, stayed there the longest, and so the bond between us was greater. She took me to the induction center when I was drafted into the army, and she wept at my departure. She welcomed me back with open arms when my military service was over two years later. She traveled all the way from Washington, DC, to Buffalo, New York, to be at my wedding. She was always there for me, and she has a special place in my heart.

9. Clara Feaster was my wife's mother. There are not enough words in my vocabulary to fully describe how wonderful she was, so I'll borrow some words from the Bible. In the book of Proverbs, King Lemuel talks about a virtuous woman who possessed some extraordinary qualities. Mrs. Feaster exemplified every one of those qualities and virtues. She was very intelligent and possessed great leadership abilities, which she used to serve her church in a voluntary capacity. She was a very industrious woman who worked hard on her job, managed her money wisely, and made shrewd investments that paid huge dividends. She was skilled with her hands and made many fine pieces of clothing for herself and for her daughters. Because of her vast experience, great intelligence, and keen insights, she was able to give wise counsel to those who sought her advice. Her life and character were exemplary and provided an example that other women would do well to emulate. In spite of her great intellect and other talents, she was down to earth and was a very approachable person. Anyone could laugh and talk with her about anything. She was equally comfortable talking to those who were well educated and those who had only a limited education, and with those who were well off financially and those who had only meager resources. Everyone felt comfortable with her. When King Lemuel gave his description of a virtuous woman, he must have had someone in mind who was exactly like Mrs. Feaster.

10. The last person in my long line of great mothers is Martha Dockery. Mrs. Dockery was a good-hearted person who had always been a good friend of our family. To console me and my wife when my mother-in-law died, Mrs. Dockery came to us and said that she would fill the role of mother for us, and she was true to her word. She kept in touch with us by phone, and once a year my family would travel to Buffalo to visit with her in her home. She was always a delight to be with and was just what we needed at that time.

What a blessing it has been for me to have so many mothers in my life. I almost feel sorry for those who only have one. Every one of those wonderful women came into my life at a critically important time for me, and each gave me something that the others could not give. If I had stayed with only one mother, I would be a totally different person than who I am today. God was doing a unique work in me that required a team of mothers to accomplish.

One of God's greatest gifts to the human race is a female's maternal instincts and capacity to nurture children and give love unselfishly. Because of that gift, I not only survived a very chaotic childhood, but I thrived and am who I am today. I honor all mothers everywhere, but I pay a special tribute to this group of ten who were specially selected for me by God. God's unseen hand was made visible through their lives.

Endnotes

[Note: Statements enclosed in brackets are the author's comments.]

[1] See the following references for more information on how the Sabbath day was changed from Saturday to Sunday and how the change became canon law: *Liber de Computo* (in Latin) by Rabanus Maurus, chapter xxvii; Migne's *Patro Louia*, volume cvii, column 682; *Declericorum Institutione*, Book II, chapter xlvi; and Migne's *Patrologia Latina*, volume cvii, column 361.

[2] Canon 29 of the decree issued by the Council of Laodicea reads as follows: "Christians shall not Judaize [observe Jewish customs] and be idle on Saturday, but shall work on that day; but the Lord's day they shall especially honor, and, as being Christians, shall, if possible, do no work on that day. If, however, they are found Judaizing, they shall be shut out [Greek: anathema] from Christ" (Abe Aefele, *A History of the Christian Councils*, Vol. 2, 316; 9 BC 879).

Another place where the Catholic Church acknowledges that it changed the Sabbath day to Sunday is in its catechism. The following statement is from Section 2, Article 3 of *The Catechism of the Catholic Church* (1994 edition paraphrased for clarity):

"Sabbath – fulfillment of the Sabbath. Sunday is expressly distinguished from the Sabbath. Sunday follows the Sabbath day chronologically every week. For Christians, ceremonial observance of Sunday replaces the observance of the Sabbath.... The Sabbath day represented the completion of the first creation and has been replaced by Sunday, which represents the new creation inaugurated by the resurrection of Christ....

Page 50 in the 1957 edition of *The Convert's Catechism of Catholic Doctrine* provides the following questions and answers:

> Q: Which is the Sabbath day?
> A: Saturday.
>
> Q: Why do we observe Sunday instead of Saturday?
> A: We observe Sunday instead of Saturday because the Catholic Church transferred the solemnity from Saturday to Sunday.

In a book called *Faith of Our Fathers* (1978:108), Cardinal James Gibbons makes the following statement:

"... you may read the Bible from Genesis to Revelation, and you will not find a single line authorizing the sanctification of Sunday. The scriptures enforce the religious observance of Saturday, which we never sanctify."

[That statement by the Cardinal is a blatant admission that there is no biblical basis for changing the Sabbath day from Saturday to Sunday, and that the Catholic Church arbitrarily made the change without being authorized by scriptures or by God.]

[The following is a series of statements and claims made by officials of the Catholic Church. I am sure that you will be as shocked as I am at the audacity of some of the claims that are made by the Catholic Church. In one statement, for example, an official says that the authority of the Catholic Church is superior to that of the Bible. That attitude apparently allows them to change God's commandments and anything else written in the scriptures. In yet another statement made by Catholic officials, the pope is said to be in the place of God on the earth, which, I suppose, is what makes him and his decrees infallible.]

2.1 On September 1, 1929, the following statement appeared in the *Catholic Record*: "Sunday is our mark of authority.... The [Catholic] Church is above the Bible, and this transference of the Sabbath observance is proof of that fact."

2.2 Pope Leo XIII made the following declaration regarding the papacy: "We [the popes] hold upon this earth the Place of God Almighty."

[I am stunned that no one seems to have a problem with such an outrageous claim by the pope. The only ones who hold the place of God upon this earth are Jesus Christ and the Holy Spirit.]

2.3 To illustrate the inflated view that Catholics have of the pope, I include here the definition of the word "pope" as found in *Ferrari's Ecclesiastical Dictionary*: "The Pope is of so great dignity and so exalted that he is not a mere man, but as it were God, and the vicar of God."

[None of the apostles would have dared to make such a claim. To my knowledge, this definition of the word "pope" has not been disputed or disavowed by any Catholic official.]

2.4 In yet another admission that the Catholic Church changed God's Sabbath day to Sunday, C. F. Thomas makes the following statement: "Of course the Catholic Church claims that the change was her act ..., and the act is a mark of her ecclesiastical power and authority in religious matters."

That statement appeared in a letter by C. F. Thomas, Chancellor of Cardinal Gibbons, on October 28, 1895.

2.5 The following statement appeared in the *American Catholic Quarterly Review* for January of 1883: "Sunday [as a day of worship and rest] ... is [a] pure creation of the Catholic Church."

2.6 During a lecture in Hartford, Kansas, on February 18, 1884, a Catholic priest named T. Enright, CSSR, made the following statement regarding the Catholic Church's authority to change the scriptures: "I have repeatedly offered $1,000 to anyone who can prove to me from the Bible alone that I am bound to keep Sunday holy. There is no such law in the Bible. It is a law of the holy Catholic Church alone. The Bible says, 'Remember the Sabbath day to keep it holy.' The Catholic Church says: 'No. By my divine power, I abolish the Sabbath day and command you to keep holy the first day of the week.' And lo: The entire civilized world bows down in a reverent obedience to the command of the holy Catholic Church." [It is truly amazing that Christians, however unwittingly, have chosen to obey the commandments of men rather than the commandments of God.]

2.7 S. C. Mosna, *Storia della Domenica* (1969): 366, 367: Not the creator of the universe in Genesis 2:1–3, but the Catholic Church "can claim the honor of having granted man a pause to his work every seven days."

2.8 The following is a statement from "The Question Box" as found in The Catholic Universe Bulletin, August 14, 1942:

"The (Catholic) Church changed the observance of the Sabbath to Sunday by right of the divine, infallible authority given to her by her Founder, Jesus Christ." [Author's note: Jesus gave no one any such authority to change God's Ten Commandment law.] The statement from the above-mentioned publication continues as follows: "The Protestant claiming the Bible to be the only guide of faith has no warrant for observing Sunday." [Here they admit that the Bible does not authorize changing the Sabbath day.] In this matter, the Seventh-day Adventist Church is the only consistent Protestant [i.e., ones who adhere strictly to the Scriptures].

[3] The treatise by James Cardinal Gibbons was published in a larger publication under the title *The Cross and the Flag, Our Church and Country*, 24, 25; 9 BC 885.

We invite you to view the complete
selection of titles we publish at:

www.TEACHServices.com

Scan with your mobile
device to go directly
to our website.

Please write or email us your praises, reactions, or
thoughts about this or any other book we publish at:

P.O. Box 954
Ringgold, GA 30736

info@TEACHServices.com

TEACH Services, Inc., titles may be purchased in bulk for
educational, business, fund-raising, or sales promotional use.
For information, please e-mail:

BulkSales@TEACHServices.com

Finally, if you are interested in seeing
your own book in print, please contact us at

publishing@TEACHServices.com

We would be happy to review your manuscript for free.

www.ingramcontent.com/pod-product-compliance
Lightning Source LLC
Chambersburg PA
CBHW081841170426
43199CB00017B/2801